Staten Island

GATEWAY TO NEW YORK

Staten Island
GATEWAY TO NEW YORK

Dorothy Valentine Smith

CHILTON BOOK COMPANY
Philadelphia New York London

Copyright © 1970 by Dorothy Valentine Smith
First Edition
All rights reserved
Published in Philadelphia by Chilton Book Company
and simultaneously in Ontario, Canada,
by Thomas Nelson & Sons, Ltd.
ISBN   0-8019-5488-6
Library of Congress Catalog Card Number 76-128869
Designed by Harry Eaby
Manufactured in the United States of America
by Vail-Ballou Press, Inc.

*To My Mother and Father
who also loved
Staten Island and its People*

PREFACE

The isolation was ended in November, 1964. The beautiful island at the gateway of New York, the city's last frontier, the stepchild of New York, was joined to Bay Ridge in Brooklyn by the world's longest suspension bridge.

Months before traffic began moving across the Verrazano–Narrows Bridge, Staten Island was the target of comment and conversation, an object for land speculation and a place to explore. Visitors took the five-cent ferry ride across the Bay, many of them supplied with pads, pencils and cameras to delve for material. Their published descriptions were numerous and entertaining; entertaining to those who were being introduced to the Island, entertaining to those who knew it well because of the fantastic reactions evoked and interpretations presented.

The population began to explode. Thousands came to establish homes; some, business people in Manhattan by day, commuting back to Staten Island at night to start another "bedroom borough." Others came for land for speculating and developing and for a quick profit.

Despite its former "isolation," Staten Island and its people have had close ties for more than three centuries with people and events throughout the world, a relationship probably unsurpassed by any other area covering only 57 square miles. In claiming fame the Island can also claim a variety of "firsts."

It was the site of the first distillery, first peace conference held in America, the first national headquarters of the Republican Party and the only place this side of the Atlantic where an investiture of a Knight of the Order of the Bath was held. It's the place where lawn tennis was first played in this country and where the first tennis tournament was held. The oldest continually fortified post in America is on the Narrows and the top of its Todt Hill is the highest point on the coast from Maine to Florida.

The Island has been a haven and a home for many, ranging from the family of a President of the United States, two of our country's Vice Presidents, a dethroned Emperor of Mexico, a liberator of Italy, the first native-born American beatified by the Roman Catholic Church, as well as many inventors, scientists, poets, editors, artists, and scores of naval and army heroes.

Nor is the Island's glory only in its past. A glorious future beckons, they say. Meanwhile city, state and national officials and agencies wrangle and plan to save—they hope—the Island's great natural beauty from a harsh fate already looming from the activities of rapacious land speculators and developers whose bulldozers snort and roar gouging out hills and trees. Each day brings more and wider bulldozer desolation, followed by the building of houses, row after row and street after street of ugly, mongrel architecture.

Staten Island has been dubbed New York's last suburban frontier. Is it destined to degenerate into just another brick-and-plate-glass jungle, another convenient "bedroom borough" for the city, a suburban straggle? Or is there still time to save what beauty there is left?

Today is only a thin layer above the subterranean rivers of the past. Tomorrow is unknowable.

Dorothy Valentine Smith

STATEN ISLAND

CONTENTS

PART 1

The Dolphin and the Half Moon

Keeping sail on the *Dolphin* only during the day and riding at anchor throughout the night, the little ship commanded by Giovanni da Verrazano, the Italian navigator in the service of the King of France, had coasted along the eastern shore of North America for many days, ever searching for that elusive passage to Cathay and the riches of the Indies.

On a bright morning in mid-April, 1524, finding, between steep hills, what seemed to be a large river emptying into the sea, the intrepid captain decided to take the *Dolphin's* small boat through those narrows to see what lay beyond.

Using his spyglass, he saw that the hills on both sides of the entrance were alive with copper-skinned natives, bedecked in feathers of varicolored birds. Some came paddling out in canoes, shouting their evident delight and welcome as the explorers ventured more than a mile into what appeared to be a beautiful lake. But suddenly a violent wind swept in from the sea and Verrazano ordered an immediate return to the *Dolphin.*

Later he recorded his regret on leaving since the region seemed "so commodious and delightful. . . ."

And later, exactly 440 years and seven months later, this

brief visit of the valiant navigator was duly remembered during a tremendous ceremony when the longest suspension bridge in the world—the Verrazano-Narrows Bridge—was opened formally, linking those steep hills where long ago red men had stood in awe and wonder, watching a strange, white bird rising out of the horizon and moving slowly and steadily toward their shores.

Another explorer came the next year: Estavan Gomez, a Spanish captain, also searching for the elusive passage to Cathay. And, by 1540, records indicate that other skippers—including several who were French—had gone through the Narrows and up the "River of the Steep Hills" where, in the eleventh century, the ships of Norsemen or Vikings had been held frozen in ice near the present site of Albany.

But it was Henry Hudson, an Englishman sailing for the Dutch—who came through the Narrows on the *Half Moon* on September 11, 1609—as well as other hardy captains sailing for the Dutch—that ultimately resulted in the Dutch claiming the territory as New Netherland, with boundaries that stretched from New England on the northeast and Canada on the north, to Virginia on the southwest, the ocean on the coast and inland boundaries that were limitless and unknown.

Hudson had been cautious when he dropped anchor in the Lower Bay on September 3, 1609. His *Half Moon,* listed as a Dutch galiot of 80 tons, two-masted and square-rigged, had a Dutch and English crew of twenty men. Next day, soundings were taken before the captain ventured closer to shore and anchored near the Narrows. The ship's longboat with the mate and four crewmen was then sent out for further soundings. Later they returned loaded with fish, including ten great mullets and an enormous ray or starfish, so heavy there was difficulty getting the catch aboard.

Natives soon paddled out to the *Half Moon* in welcome, clambered over the rail and presented green tobacco, for which they were given knives and beads. Soundings and barterings continued for several days; then John Coleman, in a sounding party returning to the ship at dusk, was killed by "an arrow shot into his throat" by Indians in a canoe sending a flight of arrows at the sailors.

Savages visiting the *Half Moon* next day denied all knowledge of Coleman's killing but Hudson was wary and didn't take his ship through the Narrows till the eleventh of September, a fair and hot day. The mate, Robert Jouet, recorded: "The people of the country came aboard us, making show of love, and gave us tobacco and Indian wheat, and departed that night; but we durst not trust them."

Hudson slowly moved up the bay and then the broad river northward, hoping to find the passage to the East. But, when the river finally narrowed he turned back and by the fourth of October, having filled his water casks, and with bales of furs below deck, sailed through the Narrows on the return voyage to report his findings to the Netherlands East India Company.

The unnamed island at the left of the gateway to the beautiful harbor was left undisturbed and uninhabited by white men for nearly thirty years following Hudson's visit: its only contact with the world of Europeans and traders being when the outbound ships stopped, as had Hudson's, to fill their casks with the fresh, sweet water that bubbled plentifully from a spring near the shore. This area soon became known as the "Watering Place" for all who put out to sea.

The Patroons

As early as 1614, several Amsterdam merchants, their business instincts roused by reports brought back by fur traders and explorers, asked for and received a charter from their High Mightinesses, the States-General in the Hague, which granted them exclusive trade in New Netherland for three years. Later the States-General approved the establishment of the Dutch West India Company, issuing a charter in 1621. This charter provided an enormous operations area, with a monopoly to trade between Dutch ports and the west coast of Africa and all the coasts of America.

The new company also had tremendous administrative power. With the exception of declaring war it had complete control over its territories, the appointment and removal of officers, enactments of laws, establishment of courts and conduct of affairs with the "Barbarians." The Company's administrator and representative in the projected colonization held the title of Director General of the Province.

The Company's first group of permanent settlers arrived in the spring of 1623. They landed on Manhattan Island from the ship *New Netherland*, thankful to step upon firm earth at last.

Some months later, after two shiploads of cattle, horses, sheep and farm implements had been put ashore, the settlement was actually established.

These colonists had left Holland where life was generally good, where person and property were secure, and where religious toleration and comfortable living were enjoyed. Ambition, or the desire for adventure, lured many to the Dutch West India Company's new colony in spite of the perils and discomforts of an ocean crossing that required from six weeks to three months.

As a further lure for greater growth of its colony, the Company issued a Charter of Privileges and Exemptions in 1629, permitting any member of the Company meeting the requirements to become a patroon with complete manorial privileges. This required bringing over, within the following four years, fifty adults and establishing them in a separate settlement anywhere in New Netherland.

The patroon would be lord of his manor. He had trading rights and tax exemptions. He could bequeath the manor to his heirs. He had within his thousands of acres exclusive rights of hunting and fishing and could bestow these rights on whomsoever he wished. As his own chief magistrate, he held manorial court. He was responsible for clearing the land, erecting farm houses and buildings and providing tools and cattle for his people. They, in turn—as his colonists or tenants—bound themselves for a definite period of time, paid the patroon a rent in stock and produce, ground all grains at the patroon's mill and turned over a percentage of their increase of cattle and crops.

The first patroonships, three in number, were granted in the summer of 1630. All of Staten Island—so designated to honor the *Staaten* or States-General in Holland—and the land covering the present area of Bayonne, Jersey City and Hoboken went to Michael Pauw, Lord of Achtienhoven and a wealthy director of the Company.

While Pauw did set up a colony, it was not on Staten

Island: there is no record extant of his occupying the Island or of doing anything with it. Few present-day Islanders are aware that the only recognition of the Island's first patroon is Pauw Street, a block-long street in New Brighton on the North Shore linking York Avenue and Jersey Street.

Pauw's experience with the Indians and the trouble and expenses that mounted with this colony finally forced him, in 1637, to sell his patroonship back to the West India Company for a total of 26,000 guilders.

Although 1637 is the date recorded for the sale of Pauw's patroonship, it was on August 13, 1636, that David Pieterszen De Vries, while on a visit to New Amsterdam, asked the Director General of the province, the new Governor Wouter Van Twiller, "to put Staten Island down in my name, intending to form a colony there which was granted."

De Vries was a man of considerable fame. He was a merchant skipper, traveler, Master of Artillery in the service of the United Provinces, and one of the nineteen directors of the Company. The name "De Vries" means "the Frisian," and the achievements of David Pieterszen are still treasured and displayed in the museum in Hoorn, in north Holland.

From early youth in Amsterdam De Vries had been trained in merchandising and in overseas trade. In his early twenties, as owner and commander of a 400-ton ship mounting eight guns, he had sailed to Newfoundland for a cargo of cod, which brought a handsome financial return when sold in Spain. He had defeated pirates off Cartagena and the Duc de Guise had engaged him to fight the Turks. His longest voyage was a three-year expedition to the East Indies. On his return in 1630, with other directors, he had founded a patroonship colony on the South (Delaware) river, set up as a base for whale fishing as well as for tobacco raising and other agricultural ventures. A hogshead of fish oil brought sixty guilders and De Vries and the other directors of equal rank in this patroonship anticipated a handsome return.

But the colony on New Netherland's southernmost boundary was soon wiped out by the Indians so De Vries set forth on other ventures, helping to form a colony on the coast of Guiana.

Although his experiences with the Company's officials at Manhattan Island had convinced him that they were "a pack of fools fit only for drinking," on his return to Amsterdam he set about his plans for the voyage to his new patroonship on Staten Island.

While De Vries was deep in completing his arrangements in Amsterdam and recruiting colonists of superior quality, the Company announced a new and more lenient policy concerning monopolies. Henceforth, the fur trade and the privilege of holding and cultivating land would be open to anyone, including foreigners. What regulations remained were few and moderate.

There were other inducements to attract potential colonists. For a term of six years the colonist would be provided with a farm of a size for easy cultivation and profit, along with a house, a barn, four horses, four cows, sheep, swine and necessary equipment. If needed, clothes and other necessaries would be provided on credit. The settler's obligation was an annual rental in money and 80 pounds of butter. At the end of six years the equivalent of the original livestock received had to be restored, though all increase of animals over the original number belonged to him.

On September 25, 1638, De Vries set sail with his colonists. His journal records that he and "some persons in my service" went aboard the Company ship, *DeLiefde*, and, on the same day, weighed anchor and set sail with some ships bound for Spanish ports and Gibraltar.

A Dunkirk frigate attacked three days later but was beaten off. The long voyage settled down, finally, after they passed Madeira. Their next sight of land was not until the eighth of November when De Vries saw a West Indian island and they hove to in the port of St. Christopher for fresh food supplies and water.

More than six weeks of gales and heavy seas lay ahead; then, running up the coast the day after Christmas, De Vries told the captain that they were close to Sandy Hook. After scanning the distant shore through the glass the captain reported in disgust that the land was covered with snow. The warmth of the West Indies was far more attractive than the cold and whiteness that stretched ahead and the captain urged that they go back there to pass the winter. He then, De Vries recorded, "solicited me to pilot the ship in, which I did. . . ."

"I brought the ship that same evening before Staten Island," De Vries noted with satisfaction, "which belonged to me, where I intended to settle my people and, in the dark, let our anchor fall in eight fathoms."

Next morning there was a heavy fog blanketing the harbor but De Vries was not deterred and took the little ship up the bay to Manhattan Island, dropping anchor opposite the fort. They were "received with much joy, as they did not expect to see a vessel at that time of year. . . ."

De Vries stayed at New Amsterdam for eight days with his people, meeting the new governor, William Kieft (a vast improvement, in his opinion, over Van Twiller), and completing the final business of taking over his patroonship. They came down the bay on January 5, 1639, put in at the Watering Place and went ashore "to plant a colony there and build."

The new Patroon was familiar with the Watering Place, having on previous departures from New Amsterdam stopped —as did all other vessels leaving the harbor—to fill the ship's casks with the sweet, spring water flowing down to the shore. This would be the site of his first settlement. Along with the assurance of a fine water supply, the surrounding land was open and level, needing only a little effort for clearings for the first plantings. Roofed-over dugouts thatched with reeds, similar to those first used on Manhattan, could provide shelter while the timber was readied for houses and barns and the land was cleared for the first crops of tobacco and maize. Game from the woods, fish and oysters from the bay, along with supplies brought over from Manhattan, would keep their stomachs satisfied. Much labor lay ahead but the rewards promised to be rich and gratifying.

Wars: Pig, Peach and Whisky

De Vries made no mention in his journal that the natives welcomed his people as they ventured ashore at the Watering Place, but he must have known that there were less than a hundred Indians then living on the Island.

They were Algonkins or Delaware Indians of the Unami band, which included three tribes: Tappans, Hackensacks and Raritans. Contemporary records described these natives as being of ordinary stature, strong and broad shouldered. To men such as De Vries, familiar with the coast of South America, they looked like Brazilians in color, or like tawny gypsies often seen wandering about Holland.

These savages were nimble of foot, perceptive, of few words, often treacherous and vindictive, but brave. To a man as fastidious as De Vries they were extremely dirty and slovenly in their habits.

Both men and women covered their nakedness with a piece of coarse cloth called "duffels" or with deerskin or elk hide. Some wore a kind of doublet made of bearskins. Others had the skins of raccoons, wildcats, wolves or beaver fashioned into a kind of coat. Deer or elk skins protected their feet and legs. Some of the savages adorned themselves with strings of wampum (beads made from shells) as well as with "long deer hair, dyed red, in ringlets to encircle the head." They relished food from the sea and woods. Dogs, badgers, snakes, frogs, maize bread and a porridge of maize called *sappaen* were also among their delicacies. De Vries' people savored fish and oysters caught along the shore and game from the nearby woods. *Sappaen* was a staple that they all enjoyed.

Although De Vries had been pleased to find that affairs had improved under the new governor, he soon grew uneasy when he heard of Kieft's harsh treatment of the Indians. He was well aware that such treatment promised eventual trouble and strife.

As months passed, De Vries' annoyance with the Company mounted, especially when the extra settlers and supplies promised him never came. After a year and two days of frustration over his little colony at the Watering Place, he leased that area to one of his men, Thomas Smythe, an Englishman. Determined, however, to prosper in spite of the Company's failure to meet its obligations, he set up other plantations. One was on Manhattan Island, a few miles above the fort; the other, on 600 acres in a fertile valley at Tappan on the Hudson. He named this "*Vriesendael*."

Smythe, as leasee on Staten Island, raised good crops of maize and added to the number of cattle and swine. Unfortunately, it was the swine that brought about a bloody massacre (known as the Pig War), which ultimately wiped out the Island's first colony.

On a hot and dark night in July, 1640, hogs owned by the Patroon and the Company were stolen at the Watering Place. Not only were the hogs taken, but the watch house nearby was also robbed and the yacht, *deVrede,* anchored offshore was "attacked" and other "trespasses committed."

Kieft accused Raritan Indians living near a small river, "about five miles behind Staten Island," of the thievery and sent an armed force of one hundred men to demand satisfaction. These troops, hot for plunder and killing, soon got out of control. They disobeyed orders, fired on the Indians, killed several, captured the chief's brother and tortured him savagely.

Although the Dutch later paid 80 fathoms of *sewan* as recompense to the Indians, De Vries knew that the Raritans would never forget such wanton cruelty, especially since they had denied all guilt in stealing the hogs. He feared a swift reprisal.

Added to the Patroon's concern had been the arrival of the ship, *Oak Tree,* on August 20, 1641, with "a person named Malyn [Melyn] who said that all Staten Island belonged to him, that it was given by the directors to him. . . ."

Although utterly outraged at his further betrayal by the Company directors, there had been no time for De Vries to take any action before the Raritans attacked his little settlement on the first of September, slaughtering his people and livestock, and burning all the buildings to ashes.

Would the soldiers come now to fight for the killing of the Patroon's people as they had for the hogs? This was the Indians' challenge.

Records indicate that De Vries doubted that the Raritans ever had stolen the pigs. He knew that they were "cunning enough," but he also knew that they would do no harm if no harm was done them. He agreed with the Raritans' accusation that Company servants had stolen the swine. Mournfully, he wrote in his journal that his colony on Staten Island had been "smothered at its birth."

While De Vries seethed over his losses and betrayal, Kieft asked permission for Cornelis Melyn "to go upon the point of Staten Island, where the maize land lay, saying he wished to let him plant it."

De Vries agreed to this request so long as his claim to the Island was "not prejudiced." He also gave permission for soldiers to be posted at the point where they could signal with a flag to the fort at Manhattan—six miles away—the arrival of any ships in the Lower Bay. Thus, Staten Island claims the distinction of being the site of the first semaphore system or "telegraph" set up in America.

Along with De Vries' permission to use between 25 and 30 acres of his land (near the present Fort Wadsworth area), Melyn was also allowed to distill brandy and "make goat's leather." So, Staten Island claims another distinction: that of being the site of the first distillery in America.

By June, 1642, Melyn was given the entire Island, with the exception of the De Vries plantation. As the third patroon, he commenced laying out new fields and preparing timber for a house and barns.

None could deny Melyn's qualities of leadership and courage which seemed harnessed to a driving ambition and a fierce spirit of independence. He had been born in Antwerp in 1600, orphaned at six years of age and placed under the guardianship of an older half-brother. At eighteen he had completed his apprenticeship to a tailor in Antwerp and later records show him, at twenty-six, as "a dresser of soft leather."

His first voyage to New Netherlands was as a ship's supercargo. An important post, since he was in charge of the cargo and of its disposal. Apparently he'd been excited by what he had found in the New World and had been eager to return. But his first attempt at colonization had ended disastrously at sea when his little *Angel Gabriel* had been attacked by the French. Unlike De Vries, who had been able to fight off his French attackers, Melyn had been robbed of all his possessions. Undaunted after this "great tribulation," he finally raised the necessary money for farm equipment, seeds and livestock and set out again, this time in the *Oak Tree*.

Although Melyn prospered on his Island, he chafed, as had De Vries and other men of prominence, over the Company's laxness and many stupidities, especially that of Director General Kieft and his underlings. There seemed to have been no attempt to placate the Indians. In fact, on a bitterly cold night late in February, 1643, Kieft ordered attacks on Indian encampments at Corlear's Hook on Manhattan and at Pavonia across the Hudson that turned into savage butchery rarely equaled in this country's history.

If Kieft had expected to subdue the natives, he was wrong. The tribes rose in wild retaliation, killing the white men and wiping out settlement after settlement on upper Manhattan, northward up the Hudson and inland both sides of the river. Long Island farms were also in flames.

Melyn and his people managed to escape from Staten Island to Manhattan before his little settlement was wiped out. Only ashes remained when the killings—later described as "the Whisky War"—ended.

After months and years of bickering and animosity against the Director General, Melyn wrote directly to the States-General for relief from Kieft's mismanagement. He and his friends demanded a new governor and a new system of government, "so that the entire country may not hereafter at the whim of one man be reduced to similar dangers."

Four years dragged by before the new governor came in the person of Peter Stuyvesant, a military leader, who announced that he would rule as a father does his children.

It's not surprising that Melyn and his friends were soon in bitter controversy with the doughty general, who charged them with being "pestilential troublemakers and seditious persons attempting to undermine authority."

The Patroon of Staten Island was brought to trial with a friend, a prearranged verdict of guilty was pronounced, and Stuyvesant decided to have Melyn hanged immediately. But so great was the outcry against such harshness that the Director General lessened the penalty. Melyn and his friend, Kuyter, were heavily fined and banished from New Netherland for a long term of years.

But Melyn and Kuyter were not vanquished. They took their case to the States-General in the Netherlands, where they were exonerated without reservation and given a safe conduct back to New Netherland, along with a summons to

Stuyvesant to return and explain his conduct to their High Mightinesses, the States-General.

Stuyvesant's reaction to the summons was utter rage. He ignored the summons and proceeded to wreak his further vindictiveness so vigorously that Melyn did not leave his island domain. Finally, in 1650, he went back to the Netherlands to raise funds to salvage his colony. By selling a third of his share of the Island to the Honorable Lord Hendrick van der Capellen, he was able to set sail with seventy strong, young men and with livestock and farm equipment to start anew.

But Stuyvesant was still bitter. His hatred and animosity against Melyn flared again and he attached and sold the man's property in Manhattan. Whereupon Melyn decided that henceforth he would devote all his time and energy to his island by laying out new farms and plantations, erecting houses and barns, establishing a court and "making a harbor." He was determined that his island would be "an ornament of New Netherland, an honor and credit to the Honorable Company."

Things went well and he prospered for nearly five years. The crops of maize and other grains were large. Sixteen farms flourished. There were twenty-seven buildings, including houses, barns and cattle racks, a fine herd of milch cows, horses, swine, and teams of plow oxen. At long last the Patroon was recovering his losses.

But once again the Indians went on the warpath, seeking vengeance for the wanton killing of a squaw who had helped herself to some peaches on the property of one VanDyke, on Manhattan Island. Indians landed from seventy canoes, stormed through the streets of New Amsterdam, killing some and terrorizing the other inhabitants; although for some unknown reason they didn't put the town to the torch. Their next target, everyone knew, would be the outlying settlements across the rivers and the bay. There was no protection. Stuyvesant and his six hundred soldiers were down on the

Delaware fighting the Swedes. Melyn, who had been arrested nearly a month before on Stuyvesant's order, was "in the dark hole of the fort."

By a quirk, he managed to be released and hurried home to save his people and, if possible, his livestock, buildings and crops. At least he had a few hours before the expected onslaught.

On September 16, 1655, the Indians landed, their first targets being the smaller farms. Frightened families fled into Melyn's fort-like house to withstand a siege. But the Indians' tactics were direct action. Flaming arrows and torches set fire to the roof and outer walls and Melyn and the others were forced to flee to a smaller house near the shore. Here they withstood attacks until that house, too, became a flaming furnace. To save themselves from being burned alive, they surrendered.

They escaped being tortured and killed by offering a ransom. But the original death toll had been high. Melyn had lost a son, a son-in-law and two nephews, along with several of his colonists. Fifty-one had been driven off into captivity, having been taken across the water to Pavonia while negotiations went on for their ransom.

The ransom money was finally paid. Just in time, according to Melyn, for the fires were about to be lighted for their final torture. Melyn and his family crossed over to Manhattan, "as miserable as they might well be."

The great venture had been played to the end. Stuyvesant was preparing further charges to accomplish the Patroon's utter ruin. Therefore, so as not to "perish utterly because of the bitter hatred of Stuyvesant" Melyn determined to quit New Netherland and put himself, his wife, and remaining family under the protection of the English authorities at New Haven.

And so the Dutch lost a man who believed in government by the people and in political and legal equality: the man who, it was later said, was the first democrat of this country

Van der Capellen still had the title of "Patroon"—the Island's fourth and last—but he never lived on his lands and his boweries, destroyed along with Melyn's in the Peach War, were never set up again in his name.

Oude Dorp–Nieu Dorp

The year 1661 has been proclaimed the year of Staten Island's first permanent settlement and a year-long celebration was held in 1961 in observance of that 300th anniversary. However, early records indicate that a few whites did return to the Island after the holocaust of the Peach War and were living there when Pierre Billiou—a Walloon and a recent arrival in New Amsterdam—along with Walraven Luten, appeared before the Council and requested an allotment of Staten Island lands for themselves and others who had arrived "by the last ships."

Their petition, which was presented to the Council on August 22, 1661, received favorable action, with Stuyvesant and the Council resolving "to look up a convenient place on Staten Island and lay it out for a village."

The exact date of these new settlers' arrival on the Island is unknown but Pierre Billiou as leader, along with Walraven Luten and Thys Barentsen, went to the Island as soon as that "convenient place" was found.

Stuyvesant himself identified the place in reporting to the Dutch West India Company in April, 1664: "A hamlet, not yet named, was begun on Staten Island about two years

ago and has now about twelve to fourteen families of Dutch
and French from the Palatinate; it lies about half an hour's
walk from the Narrows, there being no more convenient
place for a village nearer the water. . . ."

Present-day historians, after careful research, place the first
village or "dorp" in the present South Beach area, near the
foot of Ocean Avenue and the beach. The Governor also
reported that the village had been provided with a commodious blockhouse and, as the little hamlet was the weakest
and too far from the fort on Manhattan to be relieved in time
from any Indian attacks, ten soldiers were on duty there to
insure greater safety.

Four months after this report, an English squadron of "four
great men-of-war, or frigates, well manned with sailors and
soldiers" sailed in to make good the English King's claim to
ownership of all the lands in possession of the Dutch. The
blockhouse was seized without a shot being fired on August
18, 1664. Some days later, Manhattan's defenders capitulated
in the same fashion to the English forces commanded by
Colonel Richard Nicolls. The Dutch were in no condition
to fight. Their fort was indefensible, ammunition and gun-
powder supplies were practically nil and there was fear of
attack from New England as well as from Indians in the
north, commissioned by the English.

Later, in defending his surrender, Stuyvesant wrote to the
States-General at great length. In refuting the charge of
having abandoned Staten Island and of "quitting the blockhouse without removing the cannon" and of allowing the
enemy "to occupy and reduce the whole with fifty men without firing a gun," Stuyvesant stressed the fact that the Island
was inhabited only on "the southside, behind the hill, out of
sight of the fort. . . ."

At variance with his original report of a "commodious
blockhouse," he described it as "a small slight wooden blockhouse 18 or 20 feet square, in the center of their houses, which
were slightly constructed of straw and clapboards." The gar-

rison consisted of six, old soldiers, unfit for active duty against the Indians. The former governor gave no explanation of what had happened to the ten soldiers in his first report.

If the fourteen or more families on the Island were disturbed at becoming subjects of Charles II, they showed no outward sign. Several months prior to the capture the King had granted to his brother, James, Duke of York, all territory occupied by the Dutch and it was the Duke who had ordered Nicolls into action.

Within a very short time English place names were being used. New Netherland became the Province of New York. New Amsterdam was renamed New York and the Island's unnamed Dorp was designated "Dover" by the English, possibly because of the suggested resemblance to the cliffs of Dover on the English coast. Nicolls took over as Governor of the Province by order of the Duke of York and quickly set up his government. Areas were laid out as shires and Staten Island, along with Westchester and Long Island, was mapped as the shire of Yorkshire. Yorkshire in turn had three divisions or "ridings," with Staten Island placed in the West Riding.

On September 17, 1667, through a warrant issued by the Governor empowering the inhabitants of the Island "to chuse civill officers," Nicholas Stillwell was elected Constable. Islanders were also permitted to select "two good and sufficient men to be Overseers." The names of these first overseers are unknown, but Stillwell as Constable administered their oath. As the Island's first public official under English rule, Nicholas Stillwell had the power to judge and determine civil matters "under ye value of five pounds." Above that amount there was recourse to the court across the water at Gravesend.

Stillwell had arrived in America before he was thirty, and was called "Valiant" for his part in the Virginia uprisings and as an Indian fighter. Later—about 1646—he came northward to New Netherland, joining English settlers in Lady Moody's colony at Gravesend. Records indicate that he was "faithful and loyal to the Dutch until their rule was over." His stature and popularity in the colony are indicated by his election to the highest public office on the Island at that period.

Nicolls' successor was Colonel Francis Lovelace, who took over the governorship in 1668. It was Lovelace who, in 1670, negotiated the final purchase of the Island from the Indians; a transaction less known and publicized than the Dutch purchase of Manhattan but an equal, if not greater, real estate bargain. Title was taken by "turfe and twigg" along with a deed signed by Indian children as well as by their fathers. Payment had included "400 fathoms of wampum; 30 shirts; 30 kettles; 20 guns; a Firkin of powder; 60 barres of lead; 30 axes; 30 howes; 50 knives."

Lovelace, the records show, at a final meeting in the fort at New York, tossed in "3 halfe ffats of Beare, each of them a white six Stive^r Loafe and halfe a Mutch of Liquor" to complete the transaction. No longer need the inhabitants fear the danger of sudden Indian attacks. Henceforth, there would be peace.

The next step was to speed up immigration and growth. The Surveyor General was ordered by Lovelace to lay out lots so that "Two Townships shall be setled upon Staten Island of 40 Familyes each." A further order specified that several lots be surveyed "to compleat ye present Towne" and that the survey of the second town also be completed. Later, the surveyor laid out ten acres of meadow land for each lot at "Ye Great Kill." Grants were made on condition that the lands be improved and built upon.

That the land was good, that the timber was tall and straight, with an abundance of black walnut and locust trees, and that there were also great marshes and meadows can be read in early reports and surveys. Along with the laying out of lots, land patents of hundreds of acres for "plantacons" were also granted by the Governor. Enthusiastically the surveyors recorded that the Island was "the most commodiest seate and richest land in America."

Tradition relates that a small group of Waldenses, originally from the Cottian Alps of Northern Italy and refugees from religious persecution in Europe, had established themselves on the Island at Stony Brook, "about 1658." The place name is unknown to present-day Islanders but the area is along Amboy Road, not far from Monsignor Farrell High School. This tradition of the Waldenses and that the first church edifice built on the Island was "the French or Waldensian Church at Stony Brook" was repeated by such early local historians as John J. Clute, Richard M. Bayles, and Ira K. Morris, who cited early church records, particularly accounts left by Dominie Drisius, one of the first pastors of the Dutch Church in New Amsterdam.

Local historians William T. Davis and Charles W. Leng refuted the Stony Brook story, as did a noted group of Island authorities in 1915, pointing out that it evolved from confusion and error in translating Dutch records; that the Dutch "Walstant" had been confused with "Pays de Vaud," the inhabitants of which were called "Vaudois, Valdenses," and the like. Waldenses and Huguenots, massacred for their religious beliefs, were considered by some historians as French. That there were Waldenses or Waldensians who came to New Amsterdam by way of Holland, following the great massacres of this sect in 1655 by the French and Charles of Savoy, is a historical fact. Undoubtedly some did come to Staten Island. They spoke a dialect more French than Italian and their religious doctrines were similar to those of the Dutch Reformed Church. However, many of the so-called "Dutch" were from the Belgic or southern part of the Netherlands. They were either Flemings, who spoke Dutch or Walloons, who spoke French. Walloons from Belgium and Huguenots from France, in their religious lives, were as one. The Island offers evidence that this was true. Pierre Billiou, David D'Amareu (Demarest), Jacques Casier, Jaques Cortelliau (Cortelyou), Nicolas duPoi (DePuy) being prime examples. French and Dutch were spoken by more Staten Islanders than was English well into the eighteenth century. And, one hundred years later, sermons were still being preached in Dutch, while elderly members of Huguenot families clung to the use of the French of their forebears.

In his report to the Classis in Amsterdam, prior to the first English conquest, the Reverend Samuel Drisius wrote: "The French on Staten Island would also gladly have a preacher, but their families are few in number and poor, so that they cannot contribute much to the support of the Gospel and as our support here is unpunctual and small, there is no probability that they will settle a preacher. In the meantime, that they may not be wholly destitute, Governor Stuyvesant, at their request, has permitted me to go and preach there every two months and administer the Lord's Supper. . . ."

That the Dominie found this to be a considerable effort is indicated by his further comment that, during the winter, the journey across the bay was "troublesome," especially with "the showers and storms which occur. . . ."

By 1673, the tides of war in Europe once more lapped against the shores of North America, resulting in the arrival of a Dutch squadron in the Lower Bay on July 27.

That morning, small boats put some of the officers and crews ashore on the Island, where they breakfasted on Lovelace's sheep and cattle. A few days later the Dutch recaptured New York.

But they held the province for only fifteen months; long enough, however, for Pierre Billiou to be appointed *Schout* and *Scheppen* (Sheriff and Magistrate) and to embroil himself with several of his neighbors.

The English recapture was bloodless and quiet. A new governor, Sir Edmund Andros, was appointed. New grants from the King to his brother James, Duke of York, were made and the surveying and granting of land on the Island to more and more settlers went on and on. Newcomers pushed inland, as did some of the first settlers, clearing areas for planting crops and building homes. In the beginning most of their houses had only one room, with a loft overhead. When available, stone was used for the walls: a better material than the straw and clapboards used for the first houses at Oude Dorp, now called Old Town, since, in 1671, Nieu Dorp or New Town had been laid out near the water, at the foot of the present New Dorp Lane.

Two religious zealots, Jasper Dankers (Danckaerts) and Peter Sluyter, landed from a skiff near the Watering Place early in the morning of Wednesday, October 11, 1679. They came searching for a place to start a community of Labadists, where the teachings of Jean de Labadie, a French mystic and former Roman Catholic priest, could be followed without fear of persecution.

Dankers was the scribe on their three days of walking over the Island and his *Journal*—which was salvaged nearly two hundred years later in a Brooklyn shop and translated—provides rare and valuable information. His contemporary account shows the Island through the eyes of potential settlers and not through the verbiage of official documents. It deserves quoting in part, even though the Labadists didn't use the Island for their future communal living.

". . . We proceeded southwardly along the shore of the highland on the east end, where it was sometimes stony and rocky, and sometimes sandy, supplied with fine, constantly flowing springs, with which at times we quenched our thirst.

"We had now come nearly to the furthest point on the southeast, behind which I had observed several houses when we came in with the ship. We had also made inquiry as to the villages through which we would have to pass, and they told us the 'Oude Dorp' would be the first one we would come to; but my comrade finding the point very rocky and difficult, and believing the village was an island, and as we discovered no path to follow, we determined to clamber to the top of this steep bluff, through the bushes and thickets,

which we accomplished with great difficulty and in a per-
spiration. We found as little of a road above as below . . .
having wandered an hour or more in the woods, now in the
hollow and then over a hill, at one time through a swamp,
at another across a brook, without finding any road or path,
we entirely lost the way . . . We made our way at last, as
well as we could, out of the woods, and struck the shore a
quarter of an hour's distance from where we began to climb
up. We were rejoiced, as there was a house not far from the
place where we came out. We went to it to see if we could
find anyone who would show us the way a little. There was
no master in it, but an English woman with negroes and
servants. We first asked her as to the road, and then for
something to drink, and also for some one to show us the
road, but she refused the last, although we were willing to
pay for it; she was a cross woman. She said she had never
been at the village, and her folks must work, and we would
certainly have to go away as wise as we came."

Undaunted, Dankers and Sluyter walked on.

"We went now over the rocky point," Dankers recorded,
"which we were no sooner over than we saw a pretty little
sand bay, and a small creek, and not far from there, cattle
and houses . . . It was very hot, and we perspired a great
deal. We went on to the little creek to sit down and rest
ourselves there and to cool our feet, and then proceeded to
the houses which constituted Oude Dorp."

They found seven houses but only three were occupied.
The former occupants of the others had moved further in-
land where the soil was better. The ground around Oude
Dorp's houses was "worn out and barren."

They went into the first house, "which was inhabited by
English, and there rested ourselves and eat, and inquired after
the road."

Again they found a "cross" woman and her husband wasn't
much better. Nor was the couple hospitable. They asked
payment for the food that the Labadists ate.

By "a tolerable good road," the travelers walked on to Nieu Dorp, only occasionally having to break their way through woods and thickets. But it was growing dark when finally they saw the first house in the Dorp. "We found there an Englishman who could speak Dutch," Dankers wrote, "and who received us very cordially into his house, where we had as good as he and his wife had. She was a Dutch woman from the Manhattans, who was glad to have us in her house."

The next morning, Thursday, October 12, they set off early, even though they had scarcely slept. "We had no more villages to go to," Dankers wrote in his *Journal*. Henceforth they were to go from one plantation to another, "for the most part belonging to French, who showed us every kindness because we conversed with them in French."

They strode along the shore westward, "Finding sometimes fine creeks well provided with wild turkeys, geese, snipe, and wood-hens." Finally, they came to the western tip of the Island where they found an Englishman living alone some distance from the road. This may have been Christopher Billopp, former Commander and Subcollector of Delaware Bay, who had been dismissed in disgrace from his post seven months previously, and who now was living on his 1,300-acre grant on the southwest end of the Island. The Englishman fed the Labadists and warned them that they'd have a very bad road for the next two or three hours. The way was neither path nor road but they fought through thickets and crossed brooks and creeks until they found, in the woods, "a miserably constructed tabernacle of pieces of wood covered with brush, all open in front, and where we thought there were Indians; but on coming up to it we found in it an Englishman sick, and his wife and child lying upon some bushes by a little fire. We asked him if he was sick? 'I have been sick for over two months,' he replied. It made my heart sore, indeed for I never, in all my life, saw such poverty, and that, too, in the middle of the woods and wilderness. . . ."

After getting directions to the next farm, Dankers recorded, they continued through the woods till they "came to another house, and thus from farm to another, French, Dutch, and a few English."

From each farm they inquired the way to the next house. Late in the afternoon they came to the plantation of a Frenchman called *"Le Chaudronnier"* (The Coppersmith), who had served as a soldier under the Prince of Orange. "He was so delighted, and held on to us so hard that we remained and spent the night with him."

On the third day of their journey they followed directions from plantation to plantation until "we came to that of Pierre Gardinier, who had been in the service of the Prince of Orange, and had known him well. He had a large family of children and grandchildren. He was about seventy years of age, and was still as fresh and active as a young person. He was so glad to see strangers who conversed with him in the French language that he leaped with joy. After we had breakfasted here, they told us we had another large creek to pass called the Fresh Kill, and then we could perhaps be set across the Kill van Koll to the point of Mill Creek, where we might wait for a boat to convey us to the Manhattans. . . ."

In evaluating the religious feeling on the Island the Labadists noted: "They have neither church nor minister, and live rather far from each other, and inconveniently to meet together. The English are less disposed to religion, and inquire little after it; but in case there was a minister, would contribute to his support. The French and Dutch are very desirous and eager for one, for they spoke of it wherever we went. The French are good Reformed church-men, and some of them are Walloons. The Dutch are also from different quarters. . . ."

Such was Staten Island in the autumn of 1679. About one hundred families lived on farms close to creeks or scattered along the shore, since the water provided easy access to the city and the markets. The number of Dutch and French was about equal; the English inhabitants were in the minority.

The Manors of Cassiltowne and Bentley

Finally and formally, Staten Island was politically separated from Long Island and the West Riding in the year 1683, a year of considerable importance to the future of the province as well as for the Island. The changes began in midsummer—August 25 to be exact—when the newly appointed governor and successor to Sir Edmund Andros, Colonel Thomas Dongan, sailed into the harbor. He assumed office two days later.

Dongan was forty-nine years old, unmarried, and a member of an important Irish family. His uncle was the Earl of Limerick. Following the Stuarts into exile at the Court of St. Germain, he had become a colonel of the Irish regiment in the service of France, as well as a skilled diplomat. On the Restoration, Charles II rewarded him with the lieutenant governorship of Tangier and then appointed him "Governor and Admiral of the Province of New York." Here was a man of experience, well-equipped to take over from Andros, who hadn't quenched the demands of his people for the right to manage their own affairs in their own way. Andros had reached an impasse more than a year before when the people refused to pay custom duties imposed without their consent.

The new governor had instructions from the Duke of York

to set up a representative assembly. This he did, and by October 17 the first Provincial Assembly was in session in New York. Staten Island had one representative attending. One of the first acts accomplished by this new body was the division of the Province into twelve counties. Staten Island, ranking fourth on this list, was named Richmond after the town and dukedom of Richmond in Yorkshire, England. It was also whispered that the name Richmond was then a popular one with the King, who had bestowed that dukedom on one of his numerous illegitimate sons.

John Palmer, described as "a prominant man of the province," became Richmond County's first High Sheriff under the new government. Francis Williamson was honored with the appointment of first County Clerk. Palmer had large land holdings on the Island. As early as 1676 he had acquired part of Governor Lovelace's plantation along the North Shore after the governor had lost most of his grant as a result of the seizure by the Dutch in 1673. Palmer had been appointed "Ranger" for the Island in 1678 and he was rated one of the most powerful and important men of the province. By 1684 he had become a member of the Governor's Council.

Governor Dongan had shown great interest in Staten Island from the beginning and, when a fierce controversy flared between New York and the proprietors of New Jersey, he did his utmost to keep the Island for New York. The grant to Lord Berkeley and Sir George Carteret had given the Hudson River as their east boundary which, to these proprietors, meant that Staten Island belonged to them. But New York, as the stronger colony and through its governors, retained possession. This boundary controversy raged for nearly 150 years before it was finally settled in 1833. From it grew one of the Island's best known legends.

Dubbed the Island's "greatest historical hoax" (worthy of taking its place with little George Washington's cherry tree and Barbara Frietchie's flag), the story of how the brave Captain Christopher Billopp sailed his craft around the Island in less than the twenty-four hour circumnavigation time required to keep all islands in the harbor for New York, has been told, again and again; moreover, often with embellishments, since it was started about 1870 by Gabriel P. Disosway, a local historian, writing nearly two hundred years after the alleged race to keep Staten Island for New York.

In the 1930s, Island yachtsmen—possibly with tongue in cheek—took note of Billopp's sailing skill and raced for a cup in commemoration of his famous circumnavigation. Spectators in Colonial costumes stood on the shore of Billopp's old Manor of Bentley—known today as the Conference House—to wave a greeting to the "daring mariners."

"It was a good day," the *Staten Island Advance* reported, "it was a good race, it was a good celebration but it was bad history."

Although it was "bad history," this twentieth century race was an event that doubtless would have pleased the captain, whose career had brought him in and out of favor, and had brought, as well, lands that, by 1687, were vast enough to be called the Manor of Bentley.

That same year of 1687, after Dongan had acquired 5,100 acres along the Kill van Kull on the North Shore, his holdings were recorded as the "Lordshippe or Manner of Cassiltowne." This name came from his family's seat at Castletowne in the county of Kildare, Ireland, about ten miles southwest of Dublin. These two enormous estates—Bentley and Cassiltowne—were the only "Manors" on the Island.

At the peak, it was said that Dongan's holdings totaled 25,000 acres. Billopp's total was 1,600. Dongan's latest 5,100-acre grant covered "all the hills, valleys, ffresh meadows & swamps within the specified bounds . . . also a great island of salt meadow lying near the ffresh kills & over against long neck not yet appropriated—and all the messuages, tenements, fencings, orchards, gardens, pastures, meadows, marshes, woods, underwoods, trees, timber, quarries, rivers, brooks, ponds, lakes, streams, creeks, harbors, beaches, ffishing, hawking and ffowling, mines, minerals (silver and gold mines only excepted), mills, milldams, etc."

Dongan's Manor House, built in 1688, was framed with oak felled from his forests. Its roof was hipped. Then the largest house on the Island, it stood for 190 years, not far from the Kill van Kull, in an area whose present boundaries are Richmond Terrace, Dongan and Bodine Streets and DeGroot Place in West Brighton. The fact that the Governor had been absent from a Council meeting because he had been "engaged at his hunting lodge on Staten Island killing bears," suggests the possibility of a second refuge on the Island away from the cares of his office.

Those cares were mounting, although Dongan had achieved much for his province and its people. The Charter that he granted to the city in 1686 was one of the most liberal ever granted in the Colonies; a large portion of it remained in force and guided the city government into the twentieth century. His talents for diplomacy resulted in the English obtaining a treaty with the Iroquois Nations that provided a powerful, future deterrent against the French in Canada swooping down on the settlements in the northern part of the province.

With the Duke of York ascending the throne in 1685 as James II, New York had become a royal, rather than a proprietary, province. But the new King was a religious bigot. He had been displeased with the attitude of New Yorkers and the insistence of the Protestants to amend his proprietary laws. His orders promised future trouble, particularly the one banning a printing press in the Province. Dongan, like his sovereign, was a Roman Catholic (as were the lieutenant governor and the top army officer), but the Governor was noted for his tolerance. The revocation of the Edict of Nantes in 1685, followed by severe persecution of Protestants in France, alarmed all Protestants in New York and on Staten Island. In the following months there were rumors of papist plots that so alarmed the Island's French inhabitants— many of whom had suffered religious persecution in their old home—that some fled to their boats anchored offshore for safety so as to escape any night attacks.

By 1688, when the King, for greater safety from attack from Canada, decided to unite his provinces of New York and New Jersey and the Dominion of New England Colonies, Andros was appointed to the governorship instead of Dongan. Dongan then retired to one of his farms near Hempstead on Long Island, although he kept a watchful eye on his Staten Island Manor. Three years later, when he succeeded to the title of Earl of Limerick, he returned to Ireland. A tombstone erected to his memory in St. Pancra's churchyard in London indicates that he died there, in 1715, at the age of eighty-one.

Thomas Dongan is cited as having done more for the Island than any other colonial governor. His name still lives on the Island through Dongan Avenue and Street and Dongan Hills and his "Manor of Cassiltowne" is not forgotten, even though the name has been modernized to "Castleton." When the Island was a conglomerate of towns and villages, the town of Castleton, which covered the original manor, was the Island's finest. The name continues in Castleton Corners, Castleton Hill and Castleton Avenue; and Manor Road, one of the oldest highways, still goes through an area that once was the Governor's. His three nephews, Thomas, Walter and John, were his heirs. Some of Walter's descendants, to the sixth generation, still live on the Island, proud of their heritage.

As for the descendants of the first Christopher Billopp (occasionally he wrote it "Billop"), they left the Island at the close of the Revolution with other loyalists and went to St. John's, New Brunswick, Canada, where the then head of the family, Colonel Christopher Billopp, took a prominent part in the province's affairs. The Manor house and the hundreds of acres surrounding it were confiscated by the Americans and sold. For the ensuing 142 years the house and lands had a checkered existence with different owners using it for farming and other purposes. Because of its historic significance (having been the meeting place, on September 11,

1776, of Lord Howe, Admiral of the Fleet and one of the King's commissioners to restore peace to the Colonies, with the representatives of the Continental Congress, John Adams, Benjamin Franklin and Edward Rutledge), over the years prominent Staten Islanders made strenuous efforts to save the house from destruction. In 1925, the Conference House Association was organized to restore it. A real estate company had made a portion of the property a gift to the City of New York for park purposes with the house to be used as a museum. By 1929 the Conference House Association had custody of the house and since then has maintained it as a museum. The Park Department of New York City is responsible for the grounds, now called Conference House Park.

No longer the Manor of Bentley, the old stone house, now known as the Conference House, still stands on the hill above the Raritan Bay, looking across to Perth Amboy, New Jersey, the town from which the trio of Americans embarked early that September morning in 1776 to attend the first peace conference held in America. An important affair, even though it did not then achieve its purpose.

In 1966, the United States Department of the Interior commemorated this historic meeting by designating the house, a historic landmark. Today, thousands of visitors from all over the world travel to the house at the southernmost tip of New York state, not to pay tribute to the Tory, Colonel Billopp, but to see the place where terms were first discussed that ultimately gave this country its independence.

Dominies and Churches

Prior to the arrival of the Reverend Petrus Tesschenmacker on the Island in 1683, religious services for the inhabitants had been conducted occasionally by clergymen or missionaries crossing over from Manhattan and Brooklyn. Dominie Tesschenmacker had the distinction of being not only the Island's first resident minister but also the first dominie of the Reformed Protestant Dutch Church in North America ordained in America. With his family, goods and chattels, he settled on eighty acres of the South Shore and had his cattle mark registered with the county clerk in 1683.

But the young dominie's pastorate was of short duration— less than three years. He accepted a call to the church in Schenectady on the northern frontier, where a few years later he was one of the victims of the bloody massacre when the French and Indians wiped out the town.

Nearly ten years went by before the Islanders had another resident minister. The Reverend David de Bonrepos came to the French congregation whose members, like Dutch and English settlers, had met for services in houses or barns or in the open air for more than thirty-five years. There had not been a church building anywhere on the Island prior to the erection of the French Church under Pastor de Bonrepos' direction, about 1698. His church stood on the present Arthur Kill Road, in Green Ridge, about half a mile east of the Richmond Avenue intersection. The congregation included thirty-six French, forty English and forty-four Dutch worshippers.

Island historian Dr. Henry G. Steinmeyer suggests that, previous to completion of his church, the minister preached to the English, French and Dutch of the area in the meeting house which the latter had put up in 1695 in the area now known as Richmondtown. This was the house of the *Voorlezer*, Hendrick Cruser—also spelled "Henderyck Kroesen," "Hendrick Kroesen" and "Hendrick Cruse" in sundry legal documents—who served as lay reader and schoolmaster on occasion for the Dutch on the Island. Hendrick had been born and reared on his father's farm at Gowanus, Brooklyn. After his father's death, in 1680, Hendrick came to the Island and lived on his father's patent on the North Shore.

The duties of a *Voorlezer* in Holland were specified and as such were brought to the New World. His duties were to assist the dominie in church services as well as to ring the bell. He led in the singing, admonished any noisy ones and kept the church records. In the dominie's absence he held services by reading from the Scriptures or from a book of sermons. Since he was not an ordained minister, he was never permitted to baptize, preach an original sermon, perform the marriage ceremonies or administer the Lord's Supper. But he could conduct a school in which he taught the three R's as well as religious study of the catechism.

That Hendrick Cruser did his work well, especially in keeping the Dutch congregations's baptismal records, is evidenced by his records still in the archives of the Reformed Church on Staten Island. His *Voorlezer* house at Richmondtown, on its original site, was acquired by the Staten Island Historical Society, in 1939, through gifts of generous members. It has been restored as one of the most interesting buildings in the Richmondtown Restoration. Because of the schoolteacher activities of the *Voorlezer*, it is noted as the oldest elementary school building extant in the United States and has been designated by the Department of the Interior as a national historic landmark.

The Island's population at the turn of 1700 was about 750, 10 percent of these being black slaves. There were also a few Indians, some of whom were christened later through the missionary efforts of the Reverend Aeneas Mackenzie, who had been sent to the Island in 1705 by the Society for the Propagation of the Gospel in Foreign Parts to establish the Church of England.

This clergyman's efforts were more successful than those of the Reverend Morgan Jones who had been appointed by the governor a few years before. Along with that appointment went a tax on the inhabitants for the minister's support. Annoyed at being ordered to pay such a tax, the French inhabitants protested strongly, giving as a reason Mr. Jones' "ill life and conversation." To this, Justice Stillwell replied that the real objection was the fact that the English cleric was unable to preach in French and Dutch to those Islanders who understood only that tongue.

Mr. Mackenzie reported that he received a kindly reception on his arrival. The French, he wrote, had a church, "where they allow me to preach in the afternoons, the English having no church nor any convenient place for public worship. There are not many rigid dissenters in this country. But some few Quakers and Anabaptists. The French minister and such of the French and Dutch as understood English hear me preach, but most of the Dutch labor under some prejudice against our Liturgy, which seems to proceed not so much from prejudice or education, as from being wholly ignorant both of the form and substance of it. The few Dutch prayer books I had with me have gained some of them already to a juster opinion of our form of worship . . . The greatest disadvantage to the Church on this Island," Mr. Mackenzie lamented, "is the want of an English school, for the children have no education, but what they have from their parents' language and principles. . . ."

Two years later, in 1707, the need for an English school was met when the Society provided funds for two teachers, Adam Brown and Benjamin Drewit. Brown taught children "on the South Side, where there is a mixture of almost all nations under heaven." The thirty-year-old Drewit taught in the Fresh Kills "about the center of the Island, about a mile from where we are building our church and where most of the inhabitants are French."

Mr. Mackenzie was involved in plans and fund raising for a church building for his parish organization which would henceforth be "The Church of St. Andrew." But it was not until the summer of 1712, after seven years of dedicated ministry, that the edifice—about 25 by 40 feet—was finished and opened for worship; "A pretty handsome church of our own, built of Stone."

A royal charter from Queen Anne was granted a year later. This charter still governs the present Church of St. Andrew, on the original site but not in the original edifice, although most its walls remain.

The Queen also showed her interest and favor by giving a silver chalice and paten to the church. These were used for services into the twentieth century. They are now on loan for exhibition in the Historical Museum, Richmondtown, not far from St. Andrew's.

The charter confirmed Aeneas Mackenzie as the first minister. Thomas Ffarmer and Augustin Graham were appointed the first church wardens. Joseph Arrowsmith, Lambert Gerritsen, Nathaniel Brittain, Richard Merrell, Alexander Stewart, William Tillier, John Morgan and Epharim Taylor comprised the first vestry.

Mr. Mackenzie's rectorate covered eighteen years. He was forty-eight when he died in 1723. He left to his parish the stone church, a rectory and glebe land, as well as the Duxbury Glebe, formerly the land of Governor Lovelace, that extended for 340 acres on the North Shore. Twenty-two years after the rector's death he was still warmly remembered and revered; the wardens and vestry recording: "we can never sufficiently deplore our Loss in the worthy McKenzie."

As for the Dutch and oldest congregation, it was without a church edifice until 1715, when Governor Hunter issued a license to the Dutch congregation on the North Shore to build a church. A majority of the Dutch congregation by that time had moved into the area where, as early as 1680, settlers had sought patents. Numerous farms had been laid out along the lapping waters of the Kill van Kull, which afforded easy access to markets in New Jersey and New York. Religious services had been held whenever a dominie could come from Bergen, across the Kill or from Manhattan. By the end of the seventeenth century, there were five houses and a graveyard near the waterfront on the present site of lower Port Richmond. Because of the latter, the place was becoming known as "the Burial Place."

Their church was erected alongside the graveyard. It was hexagonal in shape, surmounted by a belfry. For their dominie the church joined with the "united church" at Cocclestown —later named Richmondtown—in a call to the Reverend Cornelis Van Santvoord. Some years later the Staten Island church arranged with the church at Bergen to share a minister, each congregation to contribute one half of the pastor's support.

During the Revolution, the hexagonal church was burned when American troops under Lord Stirling attacked British fortifications nearby. At the end of the war plans for a new church on the same site were commenced. With the need for a larger house of worship, the third and present church of the Island's oldest religious organization was erected in 1846. The graveyard is the oldest on the Island. Probably the oldest inscribed stone in existence on the Island is the red sandstone block found in 1922 when historians William T. Davis, Charles W. Leng and Royden W. Vosburgh were carefully copying the gravestone inscriptions. The stone read: "Anno 1715/ hk. G.K./ Ds Heeren."

Obviously this crudely marked stone was the cornerstone of the hexagonal church. The initials are believed to be those of Hendrick and Garret Kruse, the master builders of the church: the *Voorlezer* and his nephew, respectively.

From the time of the patroons to the end of the eighteenth century the Island's population was composed almost entirely of Protestants. With the exception of Governor Dongan, and the three English Jesuits who accompanied him to New York, there were no Roman Catholics on the Island during that period. Nor were there any Jews, despite the fact that a Jewish synagogue had been erected in Manhattan and that Portuguese Jews had lived in the city when it was New Amsterdam.

Towne Houses and Gaols

As early as 1682, the constable and overseers of Staten Island were ordered to "make a rate for the building of a strong and sufficient prison in some convenient place upon the said Island and also a Town House." However, that order was not carried out for more than a quarter of a century and then only in the building of a jail. In the interim the courthouse was wherever the justice sat; courts were held in taverns or in the homes of the constable, sheriff, overseers and other officials.

However, an entry dated 1688, in the county's Record Book, reads: "Pleas held att the Courte house of the County of Richmond for the said County the first Tuesday in December, in the fourth yeare of the Reigne of our Soveraigne Lord James of the Second King of England and in the yeare of our Lord Christe one Thousand six Hundred, eighty and eight, Before Thomas Lovelace, Esqr. Judge of the Inferiour Courte of Please for the County aforesaid, and Richard Stillwell & Jacob Garrettson Esqrs, Justices of the Peace within the said County."

Be that as it may, there was no public building, as such, on the Island in 1688. But this entry does provide the infor-

mation that the Island did have a judge prior to Ellis Duxbury, who had been commissioned in 1691. Nor is there evidence that the constable and overseers carried out the order
of 1682 for "a strong and sufficient prison." Punishment for
those found guilty of wrongdoing continued to be in the
paying of fines or other restitution rather than terms in gaol.

With the formation of the County of Richmond in 1683,
the little settlement called Stony Brook became the county
seat.

A search through the Island's earliest records discloses that
most of the legal actions involved damage suits, non-payment
of debts, "trespus," boundary lines, impounding of stray
cattle and similar controversies. These records are prime examples of court clerks following their own versions of punc-
tuation and spelling.

Typical of damage suits was Thomas Walton's against William Briten (Britten), who had "A parsll of un Ruly horses
which ofton times have Brooken my fence to my greet
dameg and like wis have neglected maintaining his fenc A
Cording to A grement whar by on Ruly horses and on soe-
fishiont fenc I hav Lost my whole Crop of Indgon Corn and
part of my pees to greet damog to the valew of 4^L. 19^{sh}. 6^d
whar foor the plf Craveth Jugment of the seam with Cost of
sut."

Of equal annoyance to Nathaniel Britten was Aran John-
sonn's behavior recorded "in A Action of trespus to the
vallew of 4^L 10^s" when the defendant's "doges" killed "hoges."
For this, "the Court ordeth the deft shall Kill his dogs or pay
for the swine with Cost of seut."

In 1704 the Provincial Assembly passed an act empowering the justices of the peace "to Assess Levy and Collect
not exceeding £200" for building a county jail and county
house since the Island didn't have such buildings.

As soon as the act was confirmed, five of "Her Majesties
Justices of the peace for the County of Richmond (Ellis Duxbury, Joseph Billopp, Daniel Locke or Lake, Ephraim Taylor

and Abraham Lakeman) being met together on the Eighteenth
Day of September in the Third year of the Reign of our
Sovereinge Lady Anne over England Scotland France and
Ireland Queene Defender of the fath & Anno Dom: 1704 and
by the Majority of Votes Made Choice of Lambart Garrison
Sherriff Jaques Poillion Gen^t and Antony Tyse yeoman for
to Looke for the most Convenient place in the Center of the
said County to build and Erect an Edifice on."

But it wasn't until late in January, 1707, that the decision
was made to build "the Towne house and preson" in Coccles
Town, at the head of the Fresh Kill. The order was signed
by four Justices—Ellis Duxbury, Joseph Billopp and John
Stillwell—with Abraham Lakeman making his mark. The site
was on land promised by Louis DuBois and Mr. Rezeau "for
the use of the County for ever."

Apparently, progress was slow. An entry in the County
book for 1710 records that, at long last, the work on the
prison house had been started under the supervision of William Tillyer, the sheriff, and Lambert Garrison, who had
preceded him. Described as a two-story building of stone,
"twelve foot in breadth, fourteen foot long" with the "Loar
Room six foot from beam to plank" and the upper floor also
six feet high, this was the gaol for the County of Richmond.

Meanwhile, Stony Brook, where the county seat had been
established in 1683, continued to be the place where the
Courts of Sessions and Common Pleas were conducted, although Court was held, occasionally, at Colonel Graham's
or other public and private houses on the North Side.

Faced with the responsibility of maintaining law and order,
raising funds to carry on their county government and in
having local ordinances passed to meet any anticipated conditions, freeholders and other Island inhabitants came together
for a general town meeting on the first day of April every
year "for the choising of such officers as are nescerary for the
ensuing year."

The Island had been measured out into three divisions:

North, South and West. Each division had a constable, a supervisor, two assessors, a collector and two highway surveyors, who were responsible for carrying out the affairs of county and division government.

After sixty years of English rule, Staten Island had not yet been favored with a public building for use as a courthouse and its jail was two miles distant from Stony Brook, the county seat. In fact there were some Islanders who murmured that Stony Brook was inconvenient. Coccles Town—or Cuckolds Towne as it was sometimes spelled—was more centrally located, they said, with roads branching from there to the North Side, the Watering Place and Billopp's; and it was easily reached by boats up to the head of Fresh Kill. Finally, those selected to make the decision took proper and final action. And in moving the county seat from Stony Brook to the new location, the more dignified name, "Richmondtown," was put to use.

Appeals were made in 1728 to the New York Assembly for authority to enable Richmond County justices of the peace "to build a County House and New Gaol." The latter was necessary because of the insecure and crumbling condition of the one erected in 1710. Although there are entries that courts had been held in the Court House at Richmondtown in 1729, there are no records extant to prove that the edifice itself had been erected at that time. The building—long sought and hoped for—probably didn't come into existence and use till 1738, as indicated by receipts for 38 pounds, six shillings and three pence, signed by John Veghte in July and October of that year "for the building of a County house or Court house in the County of Richmond."

In fact, as late as 1741, the Assembly passed an Act enabling the justices to complete the jail and County House, since the original 200 pounds had not been sufficient to finish the courthouse and the justices had no power to levy any sum over 20 pounds.

The new jail—the second for the county—put up in 1729

to replace the original 12-by-14-foot building of 1710, on the site of the present northeast corner of Arthur Kill Road and Center Street, became known as "the old red jail." It stood on the northeast corner of Richmond and Arthur Kill Roads until 1895, when it was destroyed by fire.

Tradition has it that the British burned the Court House during the war. When independence and peace were finally won, the first Court of General Sessions was held in Richmondtown on Monday, May 3, 1784, at three o'clock in the afternoon, in the house of Thomas Frost.

The Ways of Islanders

Viewed by outsiders, the image of Staten Island and its in-habitants was not always flattering, as was evidenced in 1732 by a writer who described the Islanders as "principally Dutch and French. The former have a Church, but the latter having been long without a Minister, resort to an Episcopal church in Richmond Town, a poor mean village and the only one on the Island."

The Swedish scientist, Peter Kalm, while traveling in North America, 1748 to 1751, to study natural history, agriculture and plantations, was kinder in what he wrote about the Island during his brief visit in 1748. From Elizabethtown, where his party had passed the night at the inn, he wrote, "We were brought over, together with our horses, in a wretched half-rotten ferry. . . . The country was low on both sides of the river, and consisted of meadows. But there was no other hay to be got, than such as commonly grows in swampy grounds; for as the tide comes up in this river, these low plains were sometimes overflowed when the water was high. The people hereabouts are said to be troubled in summer with immense swarms of gnats or mosquitoes, which sting them and their cattle. This was ascribed to the low swampy meadows, on which these insects deposit their eggs, which are afterwards hatched by the heat.

"As soon as we had got over the river, we were upon Staten Island, which is quite surrounded with salt water. This is the beginning of the province of New York. Most of the people settled here were Dutchmen, or such as came hither whilst the Dutch were yet in possession of this place. But at present they were scattered among the English and other European inhabitants, and spoke English for the greatest part. The prospect of the country here is extremely pleasing, as it is not so much intercepted by woods, but offers more cultivated fields to view. Hills and vallies still continued, as usual, to change alternately.

"The farms were near each other. Most of the houses were wooden; however some were built of stone. Near every farm house was an orchard with apple trees. Here, and on the whole journey before, I observed a press for cyder at every farm house, made in different manners, by which the people had already pressed the juice out of the apples, or were just busied with that work. Some people made use of a wheel made of thick oak planks, which turned upon a wooden axis by means of a horse drawing it, much in the same manner as the people do with wood; except that here the wheel runs upon planks. Cherry trees stood along the enclosures round corn fields.

"The corn fields were excellently situated, and either sown with wheat or rye. They had no ditches on their sides, but (as is usual in England) only furrows, drawn at greater or lesser distances from each other.

"In one place we observed a water mill so situated that when the tide flowed, the water ran into a pond, but when it ebbed, the flood gate was drawn up, and the mill driven by the water flowing out of the pond."

Apparently Kalm's party had moved along the North Side at a good pace after landing from Adoniah Schuyler's ferry, which plied back and forth, whenever needed, from the northwest corner of the Island—now Holland's Hook—to the landing for Elizabethtown, since he recorded in his journal: "About eight o'clock in the morning we arrived at the place where we were to cross the water in order to come to the town of New York. . . ."

The following spring, Kalm, still traveling and making notes, returned briefly to the Island. In commenting then on the great quantity of cherry trees before farm houses and along the highways from Philadelphia to New Brunswick, he noted: "On coming to Staten Island . . . I found them very common again, near the gardens . . . All travelers are allowed to pluck ripe fruit in any garden which they pass by; and not even the most covetous farmer can hinder them from so doing."

That Island farms produced fine crops for prosperous owners is mentioned often in records left by travelers. Island cattle and swine provided meat; and, in addition to the activities directed by the farmer's wife in the production of eggs—hen, duck and goose eggs—turkeys, ducks and other barnyard fowl were enjoyed as part of the family's daily food.

John J. Clute, local historian, writing in 1877 of the domestic life and habits and manners of Islanders in the previous century, noted that one of the busiest times of the year occurred in the autumn. "Slaughtering time" kept everyone busy, even the small children had special jobs. Beef and hogs were killed as soon as the weather became cold. The cutting up and corning of meat followed. Sausages, headcheese, *"rollitjes"* were made and stored. Hams, portions of beef and other meats were hung in the smokehouse to be cured with the pungent smoke from slow-burning logs. And, for those who liked a change of diet with game from the woods, it was easy to bring in rabbits or deer and, occasionally, bear.

The waters about the Island provided varieties of fish, oysters and clams. A young Scot, on his way from Billop's landing to the Narrows and the ferry kept by a man named

Corson, records the dish set before him at the ferryhouse by the landlady who "spoke both Dutch and English. I dined upon what I never had eat in my life—a dish of fryed clams, of which shell fish there is abundance in these parts. As I sat down to dinner I observed a manner of saying grace quite new to me. My landlady and her two daughters put on solemn, devout faces, hanging down their heads and holding up their hands for half a minute. I, who had gracelessly fallen to without remembering that duty according to a wicked custom I had contracted, sat staring att them with my mouth choak full, but after this short meditation was over, we began to lay about us and stuff down the fryed clams with rye-bread and butter.

"They took such a deal of chawing that we were long att dinner, and the dish began to cool before we had eat enough. The landlady called for the bedpan. I could not guess what she intended to do with it unless it was to warm her bed to go to sleep after dinner, but I found that it was used by way of a chafing dish to warm our dish of clams. I stared at the novelty for some time, and reaching over for a mug of beer that stood on the opposite side of the table my bag sleeve catched hold of the handle of the bedpan and unfortunately overset the clams, at which the landlady was a little ruffled. . ."

"Women's work" was never done. There were candles to be dipped or molded, sheep wool to be spun into thread and flax to be spun into thread. Many families had looms on which to weave but before the wool or linen thread could be spun, it had to be dyed. Bark from trees such as chestnuts or black walnuts or sumach provided a variety of colors. And, while women and girls usually wove the cloth from which the family's clothes were fashioned, there were professional weavers on the Island who worked to meet further demands, not only from Islanders but from New Yorkers across the Bay. When the housewife was unable to handle the heavy materials used for making "great" coats and capes there were tailors who went from house to house to do the work as there were bootmakers who made the rounds to fit each member of the family with at least one pair of boots or leather shoes a year. Some of the leather being used had been tanned from the hides of the farmer's cattle.

And what were the eating habits and utensils of these Islanders? Most of them ate mainly from wooden utensils, such as wooden trenchers, bowls and spoons, although the more affluent had pewter—mugs, porringers and spoons. Porringers were used in drinking chocolate, since chocolate was more common than tea or coffee as a beverage. Coffee was introduced from Turkey in 1650 but, in the 1740s, tea was a strange substance. In fact the story has been told of an Islander who, having heard about tea, was eager to try it. But not knowing how to prepare the dried leaves he took a ham, put it into an iron pot and strewed the pound of tea over it.

Islanders usually sat down to eat four times a day. Breakfast was suppan and milk. There were some, however, who enjoyed a breakfast of toast dipped into cider or chocolate. A favorite dinner dish, at noon, was "samp-porridge," described as a kind of soup, consisting of corn meal, meat, potatoes, turnips and other vegetables, with hominy. There was a snack or tea or chocolate sipping in midafternoon and before nine o'clock a meal, similar to breakfast, consisting of suppan and milk, or bread and milk or toast and cider.

Social intercourse for those who lived on distant farms took place before and after church services. Few families could afford carriages and vehicles used to transport families to church were farm wagons in which were placed rush-bottomed chairs for the passengers. Others rode on horseback, sometimes a man and woman riding on one horse, with the woman using a pillion, a cushion attached to the saddle.

Few women ever left their farms or hamlets to cross the Bay to New York or to visit relatives in Long Island or

Jersey. Their lives were truly insular. Probably some had never been farther than five miles from the family's acreage. As for the men, particularly those with boats and who earned some of their living from the sea, their orbits were encompassed only by their interests.

Green Legs

During the French and Indian War, British troops were encamped on Staten Island preparatory to embarking on expeditions against the French possessions in Canada. Provincial troops also had an important part in the fighting, New York providing its allotment of 2,680 officers and men, many of whom were veterans in other campaigns against the French. These colonials, far better than the British regulars, knew how to fight the French and their Indian allies.

Among these troops was Captain Thomas Arrowsmith's company of Staten Islanders, a goodly number of these men being grandsons of Island soldiers who had fought the French more than half a century before. The Arrowsmith company was part of the regiment commanded by Colonel Corse of Queens County, which took part in the capture of Fort Frontenac, on Lake Ontario, in 1758. The arms and accoutrements of those unable to provide themselves with such equipment had been raised by the freeholders and inhabitants of Richmond County in an authorized lottery.

The capture of Frontenac was part of the campaign carried through by Major General Jeffrey Amherst, who had replaced General James Abercromby as Supreme Commander of His Majesty's forces in America. Amherst's first objective had been the capture of the great fortress of Louisbourg in Nova Scotia: "the Gibraltar of America." The fall of Louisbourg was accomplished by a tremendous land and sea attack and was the first important victory in the war for the British. Amherst then proceeded to direct the campaign to crush the French in North America.

French warships were attempting to patrol the coast, and privateers based in New York and New England ports—whenever they could—brought in French merchant ships as prizes, growing rich on their cargoes. Island sloops and brigantines continued to ply their trade along the coast, although there were encounters with the enemy such as the one by a sloop, owned by Hezekiah Wright, with one Wagalem as master, stopped by a French 16-gun ship. That story was printed in the *Pennsylvania Gazette* of September 6, 1759. Wagalem, after leaving Egg Harbor, had been fired on and brought to by the French ship off the Delaware Capes. He was released after having been held a few hours, the French captain telling Wagalem to be off about his business since the captain had not come on the coast for "such Fellows as him."

With his army ordered to move up the Hudson, Amherst boarded a sloop on the last day of April, 1759, to sail for Albany, where the next movements were scheduled to start in his conquests of New France. By the end of July he had taken the forts at Ticonderoga, Crown Point and the Champlain Valley without a battle. Meanwhile, the strategy to capture Quebec was being projected from an army based at Halifax and moving up the St. Lawrence River.

Quebec fell on September 13, 1759. This, in the opinion of historians, was "one of the most momentous victories in the annals of mankind." By this one battle, Britain had won a vast empire—an empire that stretched over an enormous part of the North American continent.

The glorious news of the victory reached New York nearly a month later. When it came on October twelfth, ships in the harbor and land fortifications fired their guns all day in celebration; the rattling of rifles and small arms by many of the inhabitants adding to the noise. When night came, Islanders along the shore lighted barrels of pitch that flamed up into the sky as further evidence of excitement and celebration.

In a few months some of the victorious troops were returning. Presently, Amherst was back in New York where he was lionized and feted constantly. James DeLancey, Lieutenant Governor of the province, came to the Island frequently while British forces were using it as headquarters. On July 29, 1760, he came over from Manhattan in his barge to dine and spend the evening, accompanied by former Governor Robert Hunter, John Watts, William Walton and several other important men. Walton was noted for his lavish hospitality. It was said that his table was always spread "with the choicest viands, while a forest of decanters graced the sideboard and costly wines flowed free and fast."

In such company DeLancey, whose reputation as a devotee of good food and fine wines bordered on the notorious, outdid himself in overindulgence at the table of his Island host— overindulgence to such a degree that the next day he was dead.

The center of the returning army's encampment was near the Watering Place and along the East Shore, ample space for Amherst's veterans as well as for the Islanders who had served under Captain Arrowsmith and a second company commanded by Captain Anthony Waters. Amherst's journal indicates that he had set up his quarters at Colonel Dongan's. He found the men looking well and healthy. The camp was dry and good and he believed that plenty of spruce beer "will continue them in health." He ordered the troops, especially those who had arrived in transports from England, to be given exercises twice a day as well as rounds of target practice.

Islanders were invited to supply the troops with provisions and goods. They were assured that there would be room for the erection of tents or booths, without charge. "All Manner

of Things will be permitted to be sold without Tax or Re-
straint, it will only be required, that nothing be sold but in
the Market Place; and that no Spiritous Liquors be brought
under any Pretences to Camp."

The commission of General Robert Monckton to be governor of New York came on October 19, 1761, with the
arrival of *H. M. Alcide* along with the fleet of transports that
had been ordered to carry the troops encamped on Staten
Island to the West Indies on a secret expedition under General
Monckton.

Along with other orders was one from William Pitt, Secretary of State, which read: "Sir: His Majesty having been
graciously pleased, as a mark of his royal approbation of the
many and eminent services of Major-General Amherst, to
nominate him to be one of the Knights Companions of the
most noble Order of the Bath; and it being necessary that he
should be invested with the ensigns of the said Order, which
are transmitted to him by this opportunity, I am to signify
to you the King's pleasure, that you should perform the
ceremony; and it being his Majesty's intention, that the same
be done in the most honorable and distinguished manner that
circumstances will allow of, you will concert and adjust with
General Amherst such time and manner for investing him
with the ensigns of the Order of the Bath, as shall appear to
you most proper for shewing all due respect to the King's
order, and as may at the same time, mark in the most public
manner his Majesty's just sense of the constant zeal and signal
abilities, which General Amherst has exerted in the service of
his King and country, I am, etc. W. Pitt."

Next to the Order of the Garter this was the highest honor
that the King could bestow. George I had established it, in
1725, as a military order. Amherst's was the first investiture of
the Order performed in America. The knighthood had actually been conferred on the General in elaborate ceremonies
in Westminster Abbey in May, 1761. At that time, a proxy
took the place of Amherst.

"Captain Hankerson of the *Alcide* brought me," Amherst tersely noted in his journal, "my dispatches with Ensigns of the Order of the Bath."

The ensigns consisted of a gold insignia hanging by a broad, red ribbon, sloping from the right shoulder and across the knight's chest to his waist. A gold collar, massive and heavily engraved, to be worn about his neck and there was also a large silver star to be placed on the left shoulder.

Barges carrying groups of prominent New Yorkers crossed the Bay for the ceremony. Some came the day before to be assured of safe arrival. Hundreds of Islanders arrived to witness the excitement, some being important enough to have been invited to the marquee. Since Sir Jeffrey frequently wore green silk stockings—or, so it was said—Islanders had their own name for the hero. Happily, they called him "Green Legs."

The new Knight of the Bath made no record in his journal concerning the ceremony. But, undoubtedly, it was one long remembered by those who were present, whether they were dignitaries viewing the polished and pipe-clayed troops drawn up at attention or small boys perched precariously in trees. Special officers designated to bear the ensigns carried them so that General Monckton, after reading Pitt's letter, could place the ribbon over Amherst's shoulder and attach the heavy gold collar around his neck and the glittering star on his left shoulder and declare him "Sir Jeffrey Amherst, Knight Companion of the Order of the Bath."

"Sir," replied Sir Jeffrey, "I am truly sensible of this distinguished mark of his Majesty's royal approbation of my conduct, and shall ever esteem it as such; and I must beg leave to express to you the peculiar satisfaction, I have, and the pleasure it gives me, to receive this mark of favor from your hands."

The next day, October 26, when Sir Jeffrey sailed up the Bay to New York, Islanders could hear the boom of the cannon at Fort George in a royal salute.

Sir Jeffrey acquired further honors and titles—Baron Amherst of Holmesdale, in 1776, and Baron Amherst of Montreal, in 1787. He was offered command of British armies being sent to put down the revolution of the Colonies but he declined because of his admiration and respect for many of those Americans.

In the opinion of Island historians: "Probably Staten Island was never honored with being the scene of a more dignified or important royal ceremony."

PART 2

Whigs and Tories

At the outbreak of the Revolution, Christopher Billopp, a descendant of the original owner of the Manor of Bentley, and his father-in-law, Benjamin Seaman, who was county judge, were the top men in power and wealth on the Island. Tories in their beliefs, their loyalty to the King was well known. In fact, as members of the Assembly they had voted in February, 1775, against sending delegates from New York to the Continental Congress.

For the First Provincial Congress meeting in New York on May 22, 1775, a little over a month after British troops and American farmers at Lexington and Concord fired the shots heard 'round the world, the Island sent as its delegates, Paul Michau, John Jorney, Aaron Cortelyou, Richard Conner and Richard Lawrence. As part of its deliberation and actions, this Congress acknowledged the Continental Congress meeting in Philadelphia but withheld total obedience to its actions.

The Island was not represented at the Second Provincial Congress, which met in December, 1775. After sharp criticism for such lack of interest, Adrian Bancker and Richard Lawrence were sent to the May, 1776, meeting. The Continental

Congress had been informed of the tepid attitude of the Island's political bigwigs and had so recorded its displeasure in the minutes of its February 8 meeting. It also requested that the Provincial Congress of New Jersey send Colonel Herd and his regiment to the Island "to guard it against possession by the British."

Lawrence and Bancker protested vigorously, saying that the coming of Colonel Herd with his men to call the people to account for their conduct, just as the cause "was gaining ground," would have a bad effect on the Islanders.

Before Lawrence and Bancker could take their seats they had to give proof that the majority of Islanders "had subscribed to the association." There was further trouble when Bancker's request for powder for Richmond County's militia was denied "because certain formalities had not been conformed with."

That patriots also looked askance at the behavior of certain Islanders is evidenced by a complaint that they were supplying British transports with provisions. In May, Peter Poillon was arrested for supplying provisions to the King's ships but he was discharged with a caution after pleading ignorance of the regulations.

The Island's militia had been formed into four companies by the first of April, 1776. Two days later, Lawrence reported that fourteen good flats or scows were readied, sufficient for the removal of cattle and horses, which, it was feared, the British might commandeer.

On April 12, the Island's Committee of Safety received notice from Lord Stirling—commanding American troops under General Israel Putnam—that he was bringing in a brigade to guard the Island and that quarters would be needed for his men. This meant that the Committee of Safety, in addition to preparing farm houses and barns to shelter the troops, must also use "influence with the inhabitants to consider the soldiers as their countrymen and fellow citizens employed in the defence of the liberties of their country in general, and of the inhabitants of Richmond County in particular, and endeavour to accommodate them accordingly."

The people were anxious to know whether they were to be paid for firewood used by the troops and if their labor in building the guardhouse, ordered by Lord Stirling, would also be paid for. New England troops were on duty at the Narrows. Virginia riflemen guarded the North Shore. At times British small boats ventured into the Watering Place to replenish ship casks. The English Governor Tryon, who had fled to the safety of a British warship offshore—part of a squadron headed by the *Asia* patrolling the Lower Bay—reported: "We were alarmed by heavy Platoon Firings from the Staten Island shore, which by the help of a Spy glass we discovered to be the enemy firing upon the Seamen that were landed for water at the watering place under cover of the Savage Sloop of War . . . Lord Stirling, I am told, headed five hundred men on this attack upon eighteen unarmed seamen."

A lookout at the Narrows was set up to give warning of any British approach from the sea. "Washington's Lookout" it was called, probably because the Commander in Chief himself had selected the spot when supervising the fortifications for the defense of New York.

"To the Exp^n—of myself and party recct^g and sev^l landing places on Staten Island—16.10.0," he had entered in his expense account to be presented to Congress. The date was April 25, 1776.

Apparently, over a month later the General visited the Island again, while on his way to appear before the Continental Congress in Philadelphia, for he wrote from Amboy to General Schuyler that he had "stopped to view the ground and such places on Staten Island contiguous to it as may be proper for works of defence."

No written records, other than Washington's, seem to exist to prove if and where the General might have been on the Island before the British armies, thirty thousand strong, took over. However, during the Washington Bicentennial in 1932, the Island's director for that nationwide observance and celebration, Vernon B. Hampton, repeated a tale handed down in the Post family, that he had learned from present-day members of the family.

Generation after generation, father to son, the story had been told of how Washington, after stopping at the De Harts, had passed the nearby Post homestead on the North Shore on his way to cross the Kill into New Jersey and that young Ezekiel Post, then about fourteen, had followed the officers, staying with them for two weeks in Jersey.

Years later—1950, to be exact—Lefferd M. A. Haughwout wrote an article to prove that Washington had been on the Island. In printing the article in the *Staten Island Historian* of July-September, 1950, the editor of the publication noted that the article, "while controversial, opens up a new line of thought on a very old topic of discussion, namely whether or not General George Washington ever visited Staten Island. All previous historians have been inclined to the negative, which proves nothing. If we agree with the author, perhaps we are sacrificing one of the almost sacred distinctions of Staten Island that 'George Washington never slept here,' but let us approach the subject with an open mind."

Stressing the need for an accurate chronology of facts, since, "if chronology is wrong, all is wrong," Mr. Haughwout carefully followed Washington's movements date by date to prove (what he believed intensely) that the General actually had been on the Island; that the reconnoitering had not been by boat but that it had covered the East Shore to the Narrows and the South Shore as far as Prince's Bay where earthworks hastily had been flung up. Washington had arrived in Manhattan on April 13, 1776, the same day that British ships carrying troops commanded by General Clinton had appeared on the horizon off Sandy Hook.

With water approaches covered by enemy ships standing off the East and South Shores, the Island could be reached safely only from the North and West Shores. Obviously, the sole entry was from the Kills.

Further research, aided by conferences with Dr. Hampton, convinced Mr. Haughwout that a tradition in the De Hart family, carried from generation to generation for 174 years, was absolutely true. It was true that Washington and his reconnoitering party had stopped and spent some time at the De Hart house, although whether or not "Washington had slept there" has never been determined.

The De Harts' hospitality was well known. Travelers over the Shore Road on their way to the ferry across the Kills always stopped at their comfortable, old farmhouse. Three "Boiling Springs" near the house provided sweet water for men and beasts and the hearty food on the De Harts' table was always shared freely with travelers.

The Post family tradition confirmed the story that Washington and his party had stayed at the De Harts. The families were close neighbors and friends; in fact, there had been a marriage uniting the families and it was natural for young Ezekiel Post to scurry over to see the uniformed horsemen, to make friends with the officers and follow them to Jersey.

Mr. Haughwout in summing up his case wrote: ". . . it has been established that all who had any association with Washington had the incident indelibly fixed in mind and memory. The magic of his name and person made his movements, even through villages and hamlets and the countryside, significant, and something to be cherished."

The British Take Over

Although the British Army didn't land on Staten Island until early July, 1776, the first blood shed in the war occurred on April 15, when Virginia riflemen captured sailors from the *Savage*, who had come ashore to fill their casks at the Watering Place. During the rapid exchange of shots a lookout on the *Savage* firing from her roundtop was neatly cut down by a rifleman on shore. There were no casualties among the Americans but a curious Islander, Neddy Beattie (who lived nearby), coming over the hill to see what the firing was about, was hit by a spent ball. The story, as told years later, was that he fell down, thinking he'd been killed, but he soon recovered with the aid of a doctor who bled him.

The ship carrying General William Howe, commander of the British forces to wrest New York from the rebels, dropped anchor off Sandy Hook on June 25, 1776. Four days later the Halifax fleet of 130 ships joined him. While waiting, Howe had conferred with Governor Tryon and other important New Yorkers who had fled to safety aboard the *Dutchess of Gordon*, and he was made aware how well the Rebels had posted a large area with entrenchments in New York and on Long Island. More than one hundred cannon had been set up for the defense of the city from the sea and to obstruct any British ships trying to get into the Hudson. He also learned that the Americans had a "considerable train of field artillery."

Three warships escorted the British transports through the Narrows and in two days—July second and third—nine thousand troops had come ashore at the Watering Place. These were mainly Grenadiers and Light Infantry. Howe, in reporting to Lord George Germain, Secretary of State for the Colonies, wrote that the troops arrived "to the great joy of a most loyal people, long suffering on that account under the oppression of the Rebels stationed among them, who precipitately fled on the approach of the shipping . . ."

Ten days later, twenty thousand additional troops were landed, joining those who were "in cantonments, where they have the best refreshments." Clinton's men, numbering about three thousand, who had failed in their attack on Charleston, when they arrived, increased the total of fighting men to 32,000. For the Island, with a population slightly under three thousand, three hundred of these being slaves—the arrival and encampment of 32,000 troops must have seemed overwhelming. There was, of course, the bright prospect of the lure of British gold. That lure, undoubtedly caused numerous Islanders to profess their loyalty to the King. But there were also many who were aiding the American cause secretly, believing that by not publicly declaring their feelings their service would be more effective. There were some, however, so eager to fight that they went across the Kills and joined regiments forming in Jersey.

Headed by Christopher Billopp, those Islanders eager to serve the King were enlisting in four companies of British provincial troops. On the sixth of July, they took the oath at Richmondtown. Billopp was to be their lieutenant colonel, with Cortland Skinner of Amboy over him as colonel.

A few days later Howe was said to have sent out Isaac Decker—an Islander who had been proscribed by the Conti-

nental Congress as "inimical to the cause of America"—to visit
farmers and urge them to drive their cattle and sheep to the
Watering Place where they would receive a good price for
the animals. With scores of cattle being driven in, the fields
of the Glebe, lush with oats and wheat and good grass, were
soon as bare as they had been when Amherst's troops many
years before had occupied the site. In those first weeks of
occupation Island farmers were well paid in British gold for
the provisions brought in for the troops. Some of that gold
still remains, it is said, treasured by present-day descendants.

More than a century and a quarter ago—between 1839 and
1851—firsthand descriptions of those war years were collected
by John Anthon and his son, Charles E. Anthon. Over those
years, both Anthons visited and interviewed Island octo-
genarians and several over ninety years of age, keen of mind,
who still remembered those years of British occupation. These
reminiscences, along with stories still passed down in Island
Revolutionary families, provide fascinating flashbacks of those
turbulent times. The Staten Island Institute of Arts and
Sciences printed Anthon's Notes in its *Proceedings* for 1929–
1930.

Some Islanders, fearful of reprisals from the invading troops,
had fled inland immediately to the safety of isolated farms.
The wife of Judge Ryers on the North Shore had been so
frightened that, it was said, she died of terror upon hearing
that the British had landed. However, the cause of her death
from terror could be questioned since her husband was a
notorious Tory, whose future activities as a purveyor of
supplies brought him an abundance of English gold during
the years of occupation.

Those who had scurried inland found, after several days
had passed, that the takeover seemed generally peaceful. Fears
subsiding, they returned with their families to their houses
near the water. Island farmers in the interior didn't see the
King's troops for nearly a week and they were pleased to
find that they were behaving in a friendly manner, paying
for whatever provisions were needed.

Certain of the officers and men were billeted in farmhouses and barns, while others lived in tents fashioned from ship sails. The Scotch 42nd Regiment of Highlanders, after coming ashore near Van Duzer's ferry on the East Shore, marched through the Clove to the North Side where they were quartered in the orchard on part of the old Dongan Manor, then occupied by John Bodine. Shortly after their arrival the Highlanders could hear the sharp exchange of gunfire from a British sloop of twelve 6–pounders lying in the Kills off Decker's ferry (now Port Richmond). The sloop was almost blown to bits by Americans under General Herd, using their pair of 18–pounders set up on the Jersey waterside nearby. The following day, two venturesome, young Americans paddled across from Elizabeth Town and fired several rounds at the British before returning, unscathed, to Jersey. Perhaps they had been stirred into action by news from Philadelphia that the final draft of the Declaration of Independence had been adopted by the Continental Congress on the Fourth of July and proclaimed on the eighth.

On the ninth of July that news had reached New York City, where Washington's forces were massed. The great excitement mounted to such a degree that, by evening, a group of New Yorkers and soldiers pulled down the lead statue of the King on its pedestal in the Bowling Green, symbolically slicing off the head. Undoubtedly Howe had been informed about the "Declaration" by his agents. By the eleventh, a copy was being read at the Rose and Crown, a tavern in New Dorp, on Richmond Road near the head of New Dorp Lane, where he had set up headquarters. Here, while he awaited the arrival of his brother Richard, Lord Howe, Admiral of the Fleet in America, with one hundred more ships and thousands of additional troops (including German mercenaries), he lightened his duties with the companionship of the beautiful Mrs. Joshua Loring, wife of the British Commissary of Prisoners.

A young lieutenant in reporting his safe arrival to his family in London wrote on July 8 that, after roving for over nine months "from clime to clime . . . we have got peaceable possession of this Island, the Rebels having quit it on our approach." The cannon set up by the Americans on Long Island did, however, fire upon the ships moving through the Narrows. Apparently this was the lieutenant's first encounter with enemy fire since he wrote that the few shots were "the first ever I saw whiz about."

The young officer was sent to headquarters set up in the center of the Island "near Richmond their Capital, containing 10 or 12 houses. Most of us lye in Barns upon a blankett. I am so fortunate being in attendance upon the Colonel have got into a good House and have a Bear skin under me—we have taken up a few—rifles in the Woods and not having heard any shotts in the Woods two nights past, we believe they have all the rest deserted the Island. . . .

"Surely this country is the Paradise of the world. We coasted by Long Island, a perfect garden, this Island tho' infexious (inferior) to it is the most beautiful fertile spott I was ever inn, it has been a good deal over-run and eaten up by the Rebels, for the Inhabitants were more divided than any part of this Country and what they call the Tory party have been severely plundered by them. However, we have a good deal of fresh provisions and pay but 3½ d. per lb. for Beef and Mutton and everything else in proportion . . .

"Here you have Corn Fields and Orchards, some large ones of Peach, Plumbs and Cherry Trees and what wood you have affords you an agreeable shelter from the Sun that is now getting warm.

"The inhabitants of this Island are tall, thin, narrow shouldered people, very simple in their manners, know neither Poverty nor Riches, each house has a good farm, and every man a trade, they know no distinction of Persons, and I am sure must have lived very happily till these troubles. . . ."

Another officer writing on the same date, Lieutenant Colonel Mungo Campbell of the 55th Regiment, destined to die the following year while commanding the troops that stormed and captured Forts Montgomery and Clinton, also left a pleasant description of the Island as he saw it on his arrival with Howe on the third of July, "where for the first time since I left Europe I have had refreshment and repose . . . This Island the most beautiful and fertil in the world, supplys the Army, with the very Luxuries of Life, I never experienced such a Change. And the Inhabitants to a man have embodyed themselves and joined the Kings Troops with spirit and alacrity. . . ."

At seven o'clock in the evening of July 12, Lord Howe, aboard the *Eagle,* came through the Narrows and into the Upper Bay, receiving a salute from the admiral in command and the rest of the fleet as the *Eagle* finally dropped her anchor at the Watering Place. A short time later the General was piped aboard to greet his brother.

"From this day forward," wrote an English captain of engineers, "I date the commencement of our successes."

A Mighty Fleet and Army Move

Lord Howe had brought the largest British fleet and army ever to come over the horizon and land in North America. Along with these mighty forces he also brought orders to negotiate and treat for peace with the rebellious Colonists.

The first step to be taken in such negotiations was to communicate proposals to the head of the Rebel army in New York. On July 14, under a flag of truce, the Admiral's letter addressed to "George Washington, Esquire" started across the Bay. Because of this superscription the letter was not accepted by Colonels Webb and Reed, who had met the Admiral's barge halfway between Staten and Governor's Islands. Colonel Webb recorded, "on acc^t of its direction, we refused to Receive and Parted with the usual Compliments."

A British version kept in an officer's journal states: "This day A Flag of truce was sent to N. York contain^g an act of oblivion—but was not received because it was adress^d to George Washington Esqr &^{ca} &^{ca} &^{a} & and that they only knew Genl Washington—A copy of the same was sent to Amboy & Received for the Congress."

The New York *Mercury* reported: ". . . A Barge from the Fleet, appeared in the Bay with a white Flag, which was met by the General's Barge with several Gentlemen of the Army on Board. The Flag was sent by Lord Howe, with a Letter to his Excellency General Washington. But as the letter was improperly directed it was not received though much sollicited by the Officer, who, we hear, said it contained nothing of a hostile Nature. . . ."

On July 16 a second flag of truce with a letter from Lord Howe was also rejected for the same reason. Possibly to punctuate the refusal, the Americans put up two 6–pounders on the bank across the water from Brigadier Agnew's quarters near the Narrows.

To show its approval of the Commander in Chief's action the Continental Congress resolved: "That General Washington, in refusing to receive a letter said to be sent from Lord Howe, addressed to George Washington, Esquire, acted with dignity becoming his station. . . ."

The Howe brothers believed that they had finally resolved "the insurmountable obstacle" of correspondence when Colonel Webb arranged for a personal interview between their Adjutant General and General Washington for July 20. They met in Colonel Knox's quarters (the American commander "attended with his Suit and Life Guards") and talked about an hour.

In commenting on the British explanation that the "&c &" on the letter implied "everything" Washington said that they also implied "anything." Repeating that the niceties of military manners be punctiliously observed and that he be addressed as "General," he declined to accept the letter brought by the adjutant general.

Colonel Webb recorded that: "In going and coming, we pass'd in front of the Grand Battery but did not blind fold him: Sociable and chatty all the way."

Meanwhile, British engineers were reconnoitering to build fortifications and throwing up earth works to protect Staten Island from rebel attack. The most vulnerable spots needing protection were along the Island's backdoor waters, so close to Jersey that little boats carrying American raiding parties slipped easily across the Kills at night, especially when the moon was low.

On July 29, more ships came through the Narrows early in the afternoon, hove to off the Watering Place and dropped anchor. Islanders soon learned that light horse from Halifax were aboard, and that two transports carried "foreignors."

Each day more ships came in. By August 11, the first division of Hessians, under Lieutenant General Philip von Heister, was said to be at Sandy Hook; however, Islanders didn't see them come ashore till five days later. These were mercenary troops from Hesse Cassel and Waldeck. Their rapacious behavior soon caused them to be thoroughly hated by the inhabitants.

Agents and informers brought in news to headquarters at the Rose and Crown and orders went from New Dorp to command posts along the water front. Frequently Islanders watched British warships, sloops and other armed craft sailing away from the Watering Place, manoeuvring up the Bay and into the Hudson, testing American batteries' fire power along the New York and Jersey shores. Years later, an Islander recalled that as a lad he had climbed the tallest tree on a hilltop near his father's farm to see the fleets at anchor. The ships lying there with sails furled looked, he said, "like a cedar swamp." With over 450 ships, including ten great ships of the line and twenty frigates—most of which were anchored off Staten Island—this was the mightiest fleet, up to that time, assembled in the Western Hemisphere. This was a sight to make the bravest patriot shiver.

The first stage of Howe's campaign to capture New York was scheduled to start on August 21, when troops would be ferried across from Staten Island to Gravesend on Long Island. But a tremendous storm swept over the Island on the twenty-first. It wasn't until nine o'clock in the morning of the twenty-second that the embarkation of Howe's army actually commenced, when 11,850 of foot, 500 artillery to man the 40 fieldpieces, and 1,500 foreigners under Colonel von Donop started out aboard the landing craft.

From hilltops and along the shore, Islanders watched the crossing. Barges, eighty-eight of them loaded with troops, were sculled across the water in the wake of ships also carrying troops. The shrill notes of fifes, the beating of drums and the swirl of bagpipes added to the excitement. The sun sparkled on brass helmets and on the guns. Scarlet and blue coats were blobs of color among the dark kilts of the 42nd Highlands (called the Black Watch) and the green coats of German sharpshooters. Regimental flags snapped in the welcomed breeze which fluttered the plumed headgear of some of the troops. The barges shuttled back and forth all day till, finally, close to fifteen thousand men were on Long Island. That night the weather changed and Islanders knew there would be a delay in further ferrying.

Three days went slowly by until the wind shifted. On the twenty-fifth, the transporting of troops resumed with the Hessian grenadiers demonstrating their rigid training by standing at attention with shouldered arms in the barges carrying them across the water.

Meanwhile, word had sifted down from Manhattan that American forces had also crossed over to Long Island to reinforce troops already entrenched there. On Staten Island, those fortunate enough to possess spy glasses watched constantly and eagerly to see when a battle would erupt.

Patriots and Secret Agents

"There was none in our army that run so many risks and underwent so many hardships and fatigues as I did," wrote John Mersereau, many years later when he was an old man, reminiscing about the service he had rendered as a member of General Washington's intelligence service.

Perhaps he claimed too much. But then, as John Bakeless noted in his *Turncoats, Traitors and Heroes,* if the whole story of John Mersereau and the other members of his family was available, the old gentleman's claim "might not be very far from the truth."

With news from Boston that New York was soon to see the arrival of a mighty British fleet carrying thousands of troops, the heads of a number of Staten Island patriot-families made preparations to cross over to New Jersey. Among them was Colonel Jacob Mersereau, a man of considerable influence on the Island, whose speeches at Richmondtown following the news of the massacre at Boston, had so enraged the Tory county judge, that he had declared the Colonel guilty of treasonable conduct.

By the time British troops disembarked at the Watering Place early in July, 1776, Colonel Jacob, along with other

Mersereaus—John, Joshua, and another John who was later called John LaGrange Mersereau to distinguish him from his uncle, John—were in New Brunswick.

While British headquarters were being established at New Dorp in the Rose and Crown, General Washington was trying desperately to set up contacts on the Island for obtaining information vital to his defenses. But, unfortunately, the two or three patriots who had volunteered and who could be trusted and relied on for accurate information had no way of transmitting it across the water. It was not until August 20 that a courier from New Jersey finally slipped over to the Island and picked up from an agent (said to have been a Mersereau) the vital news that Howe was moving twenty thousand troops across to Long Island with field guns and that his wagon train would be ready to move within a couple of days.

The Mersereaus were now embarked on the espionage network for the Commander in Chief, which they continued to the end of the war. Young John had a defective right arm so was unable to serve in the field with troops because of his inability to use a gun, but his operations as Washington's secret agent were of the utmost value and importance. From the records that remain, incomplete as they are, John Mersereau probably did not exaggerate when he said that no one had run so many risks or undergone so many hardships and fatigues as he had.

In the beginning John had stayed on the Island, using as a courier another young fellow—identified as John Parker—an apprentice of Joshua Mersereau's in shipbuilding. Parker made a number of secret trips from the Island to American posts in New Jersey, providing much information. Then he was caught, thrown into a typically filthy British prison and soon died. With the loss of Parker, Mersereau had to take on the additional risk of being a courier. The tradition is that he would cross to Jersey on a raft or skiff, his papers in a bottle attached to the boat with a "thread." He also had a pickup

on Shooter's Island—a marshy spot between Staten Island and
Jersey—where he hid his papers under a large stone and
picked up instructions. A system of signals by lights on either
side of the water indicated when papers were hidden.

Often he was challenged by British sentries and had to
escape on his hands and knees through ditches and swamps.
The British finally began to suspect what he'd been doing
and he abandoned his dangerous operation. His sixteen-year-
old brother replaced him to a lesser degree, moving back and
forth at night in a skiff hidden by day in a relative's cellar
near the shore. Another Mersereau—Paul—picked up back
files of the British *Register*, which Washington needed, and
moved them over the secret road.

Other operations of the Mersereau network was one
directed by John, the elder, who had six agents, including
Paul Latourette, possibly Abraham Bancker and Asher Fitz-
Randolph, and "strangers." Latourette, in particular, rendered
great service by going into New York with farm produce,
collecting information, and often bringing back with him
American soldiers who had escaped from prisons there.

Colonel Jacob Mersereau, who had been accused of treasonable conduct by the Tory judge, is still remembered on the
Island for his successful eluding of a British force sent to
capture him when he came home late one evening to visit
his family in their old stone house on the southwest corner
of Watchogue and Willowbrook Roads. Whenever possible,
he slipped home to be with his wife and children. This time
he had crossed over from Jersey, hidden his boat and, following a line through the fields and avoiding all roads, he was
almost home when he saw a young Tory neighbor. Since they
hadn't spoken, he got to his house hoping that he hadn't been
recognized.

Next morning, at daybreak, the early-rising Mersereaus
could see redcoats approaching. The Colonel went out an
upper window at the back, dropped onto a shed roof and so
to the ground and headed for the swamp nearby. Soon the

British were following his trail with dogs but when the dogs met up with some rabbits off they went. After a day spent crouching in the swamp the Colonel was able to escape when the sun went down behind the Jersey hills.

With people like the Mersereaus, Washington could report to the Continental Congress: "I have people constantly on Staten Island, who give me daily information of the operations of the enemy." These were brave men. And, without doubt, the young John was truly worthy of the statement: "For cold courage he was probably unsurpassed in the Revolution."

Five Gentlemen Confer

How much Staten Islanders actually could see of the clash of troops across the water on Long Island is unrecorded. Certainly those with spy glasses could follow the first movements of the Grenadiers, the Highlanders, the Hessians and other troops as they went ashore and began probing inland, testing American defenses. No doubt, keen-eared Islanders were soon aware of the news brought back by couriers. The wind—strong enough to keep Howe's ships from attacking through the East River—also must have carried the rattle of muskets and the boom of fieldpieces as the battle grew in intensity over the woody heights of Long Island between Brooklyn and Flatbush.

On that sultry morning of August 27, men fought and died there. Some, such as the two hundred "immortal Marylanders" under Smallwood and Haslet's Delaware men, counterattacked with bravery rarely equaled or surpassed in the annals of the army; courage so great that it was recorded by British officers in their battle reports. But the Americans were forced, eventually, to retreat into their main works.

The next day brought high winds and lashing rains and

Washington's decision to slip out of Brooklyn and save what was left of his army. The escape of these troops over the water to Manhattan Island, while Howe's forces slept complacently nearby, was a miraculous feat, one that a British officer reported "should hold a high place among military transactions." Heroes of the escape were the men from Marblehead under Colonel John Glover and Hutchinson's men from the 27th Massachusetts of Salem. Despite wind, rain and a strong tide these stalwarts moved the troops across to New York with rowboats, flatboats and whatever other craft could be found. For six hours they rowed back and forth, again and again, each boat loaded to within three inches of its gunwales. Near midnight the wind changed, making the crossing easier. At dawn a heavy fog rolled in, blanketing the area. Through that heavy shroud, the last men and their Commander in Chief escaped.

In the words of General Nathanael Greene, later Washington's second in command, it was "the best effected retreat I ever read or heard of, considering the difficulty."

Meanwhile, Howe, with his commanders and troops, slept heavily, unaware that the quarry had slipped away.

The feat of the Marbleheaders and the men from Salem would forever have a glory all its own. Americans, writing later to their homefolks, said: "We killed more of them than they did us. But they took the most prisoners." Among those prisoners were Major General John Sullivan and Brigadier General Lord Stirling, an American who used a British title. But, Lord Howe aboard the *Eagle* in the Upper Bay, still anxious to fulfill his duty as a commissioner of peace, paroled Sullivan to deliver a verbal message to the Continental Congress in Philadelphia.

Sullivan delivered Howe's message on September 2. In substance it was brief: although Howe couldn't treat with Congress officially, he was eager to confer with some of its members as "private gentlemen." Congress was further informed that the Admiral and his brother, the General, had "full powers to arrange an accommodation on terms advantageous to both countries. . . ."

For close to three days Congress discussed the message. Obviously Howe had no power—nor was it his wish—to consider the former Colonies as "independent States." He was the King's representative and His Majesty did not and would not acknowledge the Continental Congress. Finally, Benjamin Franklin, John Adams and Edward Rutledge as a committee were directed to meet with the Howes, either at Perth Amboy or across the water on Staten Island.

Franklin and Lord Howe had been friendly in London when Franklin had been agent there for several of the Colonies prior to the Revolution. It was said that Franklin had dined several times with the Admiral and had played chess with Miss Howe, his sister. As soon as the *Eagle* had dropped off Staten Island, a personal letter to Franklin, written by Howe while at sea, went off with official documents and proclamations. Franklin had sent a lengthy reply which ended on a personal note: "The well-founded Esteem, and, permit me to say, Affection, which I shall always have for your Lordship, makes it Painful to me to see you engaged in conducting a War, the great Ground of which, as expressed in your Letter, is 'the necessity of preventing the American trade from passing into foreign Channels'. . . ."

But there were some members of Congress who didn't favor Franklin's further correspondence with Howe. The committee would be leaving Philadelphia on September 9 to meet at a place to be designated by Howe: the house on Staten Island opposite Amboy, or the governor's house in Amboy.

Howe, in expressing his pleasure at his approaching meeting with Franklin and the others, set the place as "at the house on Staten Island opposite to Amboy, as early as the few conveniences for traveling by land on Staten Island will permit." A boat with a flag of truce would be sent to Amboy, which was in American control, for their transportation.

They would be meeting in the old Bentley Manor house, from which the owner, Colonel Christopher Billopp, had moved his family and possessions weeks previously since its position was extremely vulnerable. British troops had been billeted there and guns were set up to cover the water. American soldiers in Amboy kept the area under constant surveillance and expert marksmen, firing from the spire of St. Peter's Church, delighted in showing their prowess. William T. Davis' *Conference or Billopp House* repeats the story of the young rifleman perched in St. Peter's who shattered the bowl from which a British officer was about to drink with others regaling themselves under Billopp's trees.

Since early July there had been frequent exchanges of cannon shots from batteries on both sides of the water. The New York *Gazette and Weekly Mercury* in its July 29 issue printed a detailed account of one of these artillery duels: "Several Cannon were fired last Thursday Afternoon, from our Battery at Amboy, at a Number of Boats from Staten Island, bound to Sandy-Hook, supposed to join Part of the Ministerial Fleet laying there; This brought on a Cannonade from the Encampment of the Regulars near Billop's Point, on the Island, which continued very hot on both Sides for near an Hour; The Boats got clear, but many of the Regulars were seen to fall, and several carried off, supposed to be wounded. On our Side a Soldier belonging to one of the Philadelphia Battalions was killed, and one wounded; a Horse in a Carriage had his Head shot off in the Street, and some Damage was done the Houses."

But all guns were silent on Wednesday morning, September 11, when a boat flying a flag of truce set out from Billopp's to meet the three gentlemen who were waiting in Amboy after their two-day journey from Philadelphia.

A British officer aboard the Admiral's barge offered to remain as a hostage for the three gentlemen's safe return. But his offer was politely declined and he crossed over with them to the Staten Island shore where Lord Howe stood waiting.

Following the formalities of greeting they walked up the slope to the house between lines of Grenadiers, described by John Adams as "looking fierce as ten Furies, and making all the grimaces, and gestures, and motions of their muskets, with bayonets fixed, which, I suppose, military etiquette requires, but which we neither understood nor regarded.

"The house had been the habitation of military guards, and was as dirty as a stable; but his lordship had prepared a large handsome room, by spreading a carpet of moss and green sprigs, from bushes and shrubs in the neighborhood, till he had made it not only wholesome, but romantically elegant; and he entertained us with good claret, good bread, cold ham, tongues, and mutton."

Nineteenth-century Island historians differed as to which of the two, large, first-floor rooms had been used for the conference. Today, the room to the left of the entrance of the old Manor House is designated as "the Conference Room."

A Hessian colonel and Sir Henry Strachey, a member of Parliament and Howe's secretary and advisor for peace negotiations, also ate with the conferees but when the serious talk started the Hessian was excused.

The polite verbiage of diplomatic usage punctuated much of the sentiments expressed throughout the conversation but underneath the words was steel that couldn't be bent by either side. The records of what took place that warm September day still remain in various places in this country and in England. These include reports presented to the Continental Congress by the committee, journals and private correspondence of the participants, and Strachey's notes with Howe's memoranda. Contemporary newspaper accounts are also available for the serious researcher.

His Majesty's government was willing to make certain concessions but it would never acknowledge the independence of the Colonies. The Americans were irrevocably set on their independence. Howe, therefore, explained that he couldn't

confer with Congress or with them as a committee of the
Congress, and he asked permission to consider them as "gentlemen of great ability and influence in the country, who have
met here to converse with me and try if we can devise the
outline of a plan to stay the calamities of war. . . ."

Dr. Franklin replied: "Your lordship may consider us in
any view you think proper. We, on our part, are at liberty
to consider ourselves in our real character. But there is really
no necessity on this occasion to distinguish between members
of Congress and individuals. The conversation may be held
as among friends."

John Adams, ever blunt, said: "Your lordship may consider
me in what light you please. Indeed, I shall be willing to
consider myself for a few moments in any character which
would be agreeable to your lordship, except that of a British
subject."

To this Howe commented: "Mr. Adams is a decided
character."

Edward Rutledge, the other member of the committee, said
that he agreed with Dr. Franklin that "the conversation may
be as among friends."

So, as friends they talked. But nothing was changed. The
Colonies, now calling themselves the United States, would
not give up "the system of independency." Howe, therefore,
found it impossible to enter into any negotiations.

"I am sorry, gentlemen," he said, "that you have had the
trouble of coming so far to so little purpose."

The conference, the first of its kind to be held in America,
was over. Howe walked with them down to the shore where
his barge lay waiting to take them back to Amboy. As they
approached the Jersey landing place, Franklin jingled coins in
his pocket, pulling out a handful of silver and gold pieces for
the sailors manning the barge. But the officer in command
politely declined such largesse. Later, in explaining his gesture,
Franklin said that he did it to show that Americans did have

hard money and since he knew that regulations wouldn't allow the men to accept the coins he was safe in offering them.

The first peace conference to be held in the young United States produced no cessation of fighting. Six years later, three of those who had sat around the table in the old Billopp house were destined to meet again. This time the meeting place was Paris and Franklin, Adams and Strachey were there among negotiators to draw up the final terms for peace.

The War Years

The Howes were convinced, at last, that there was no possibility for peace. Sir William unleashed his forces on Long Island to take New York. With no apparent superstition about the date the order was given to start the first operation on Friday, the thirteenth of September. Four warships sailed up the East River, followed the next day by more ships to bombard American troops entrenched at Kip's Bay. By the evening of the fifteenth, the city was in British hands.

Meanwhile, on Staten Island the inhabitants found it strangely quiet with probably no more than a brigade left on duty. There were, however, wounded being cared for in temporary hospitals set up in barns and tents.

In his *Annals of Staten Island*, John J. Clute, early historian, wrote: "If the history of the sufferings of the people of Staten Island during the war could be written, it would present a picture too dreadful to contemplate. Neither age, sex, nor condition were exempt from insults and outrages of the grossest character; no home was too sacred to protect its inmates from injury; the rights of property were not recognized, if the invader coveted it; even the temples of God were desecrated; the law of might alone prevailed.

"Proclamations and professions of good will and protection had been promulgated repeatedly, but those who relied upon them usually reaped disappointment. It was useless to appeal to those high in authority, for the complaints of the people were unheeded, and redress for injuries, except under peculiar circumstances, could not be obtained. If a British officer's horse was in need of hay or oats, a file of soldiers was sent to any farmer who was known to have a supply, to seize and take it away. If the officer himself needed a horse, the same method was adopted to procure one. Money, provisions and even bedding and household furniture were taken by force; sometimes promises of payment were made, but seldom fulfilled. The course adopted by the British while in possession of the Island, effectually alienated many of the friends of the royal cause, and hence it was that so many of them, at the close of the war, eagerly took the oath of allegiance to the new government, and so few adhered to the cause of the king and followed its fortunes."

Along with British depredations and thievery, Islanders were constantly in terror of raiding Jerseymen seeking booty of every kind. John Bodine was one of their victims. Bound and strung up on spikes embedded in the kitchen ceiling beams, he was tortured with red-hot tongs to tell where his money was hidden. But, before his will was broken, a British soldier heard the noise and fired his musket, causing the robbers to flee. Peter Houseman, however—whose house still stands in Westerleigh on the corner of Watchogue Road and St. John Avenue—didn't fare so well when nine Jerseymen, their faces blackened with soot, raided the house before he'd barred his doors at sundown. When he refused to hand over his gold he was killed with a blow on the head. A neighbor was also hit, though only stunned and bleeding from a deep cut. Slaves, hearing the noise, saved the Houseman children by rushing them into the kitchen and barricading the doors.

Stories have also been handed down of occasions when Island farmers, in protecting their homes, killed the marauders, either Hessian or Jerseymen, and got rid of the bodies by putting them under barn or stable floors. There were also tales of attempted abduction of pretty Island girls by British officers and the punishment meted out to them by the girls' avengers.

A householder was a fool, indeed, if at sundown he didn't have all his shutters and doors barred for safety; nor were lights ever left visible from outside since there was a severe penalty for those found guilty of signaling to the enemy.

Probably the most brutal crime perpetrated against an Island family through the more than seven years of British occupation was the murder of Christian Jacobsen, a wealthy farmer, who lived on New Dorp Lane not far from the water. Early in the War he was Chairman of the Richmond County Committee of Safety and had aided in enlisting four companies of militia to help the cause of liberty. A pillar of the Moravian congregation at New Dorp, he was largely responsible for maintaining that church as the place of worship for Island patriots after the Reformed Church on the North Side had been destroyed and St. Andrew's was in British hands.

Knowing that Jacobsen had just received a large sum of money, four British soldiers forced their way into the house at night, threatening to blow off the heads of the blacks who tried to keep them out. But one of the slaves, Bet, who lived to tell and retell the story, slipped out in all the uproar and went around the house and got through to the room where the Jacobsens were sleeping. When Jacobsen rushed to the kitchen he was shot through the chest. As he fell, the soldiers, frightened at what they'd done, ran off into the night.

But Jacobsen was too important to let his wanton killing be brushed aside. An order was given that the murderers be found and soon the one who had fired the gun was identified by Bet and was hanged from a nearby tree.

The Vanderbilt family acquired the Jacobsen farm after the Revolution and William H. Vanderbilt, son of the Commodore, moved into the old, gambrel-roofed house in the 1840s.

The Island was under strict military rule. Cole's Ferry on the East Shore and Decker's on the North Shore were designated as magazines for hay, straw, oats and Indian corn. Prices were set on these commodities. A farmer could keep from his crops only the amount actually needed by his family for food. If he refused to sell the rest, the entire crop would be confiscated. Cole's Ferry was designated as the only landing place for civilian use. An Islander could bring in rum, spirits, sugar or molasses in the amount of one barrel of each; also four barrels of salt and other articles necessary for the use of only one family. Permission had to be granted for bringing in salt. And by October, 1780, Islanders were required to have a permit to carry supplies from New York to Cole's Ferry. In preparation for winter the order went out that those having permission to cut wood must bring it in immediately for the use of troops in New York as well as on the Island.

While no major battle was fought on Staten Island during the War, there were many raids by American soldiers crossing over in whaleboats. Despite British guard and gunboats patrolling the shore it was not too difficult to slip through the darkness, attack British pickets and outposts, take some prisoners and get back to Jersey before pursuit by the redcoats. The first raid of any size by American troops came from Jersey in October, 1776.

On the night of the fifteenth, a detachment of General Hugh Mercer's men crossed the Sound under command of Colonel Griffith. Before daybreak they had reached Richmondtown and, in a surprise attack, killed two or three British, wounded a few and took off with seventeen prisoners. The Richmond County Chapter, Daughters of the American Revolution, 137 years later placed a tablet on the outer wall

David Pieterz (Pieterszen) De Vries, as Patroon, set up Staten Island's first colony in 1639. *Courtesy New York Public Library*

Thomas Dongan, "Governor and Admiral of the Province of New York," 1683–1688, did more for Staten Island than any other colonial governor. *Courtesy New York Historical Society*

The *Voorlezer's* House, Richmondtown, home of the Dutch lay reader and teacher, erected prior to 1696. *Courtesy Staten Island Historical Society*

Billopp or Conference House, built about 1680 and home of Billopps for a century, was the site of the 1776 peace conference between Lord Howe and an American committee. *Courtesy Staten Island Historical Society*

Richmondtown as it appeared in 1851. *Courtesy Staten Island Historical Society.*

Richmondtown in 1970. *Photograph by Michael Koledo*

Sailors' Snug Harbor: ". . . one of the most notable Greek revival compositions in the United States." *Courtesy Staten Island Historical Society*

Miss E. Alice Austen: self-por trait. *Courtesy Staten Island Historical Society*

The pillared mansion in West Brighton where President John Tyler's wife and children lived for more than ten years. *Courtesy Staten Island Historical Society*

An Alice Austen picture of boating and bathing at the Narrows in 1892. *Courtesy Staten Island Historical Society*

The cottage on Cross Street, Clifton, where Giuseppi Garibaldi, Italian liberator, lived with Antonio Meucei, inventor. 1851–53. House later moved to Tompkins Avenue. *Courtesy New York Public Library*

"Effingham," the Alexander mansion, *circa* 1890, is now the Richmond County Country Club, in Dongan Hills. *Courtesy Richmond County Country Club*

Ice was transported in blocks from ice-storage houses, in 1889. *Courtesy Staten Island Historical Society*

Wagner College extends along Grymes Hill. *Courtesy Wagner College*

Staten Island Community College of the City University of New York has a 40-acre campus along Staten Island Expressway and Ocean Terrace. *Courtesy Staten Island Community College*

The world's largest, aboveground storage tank for liquid natural gas. Bloomfield, 1970. *Courtesy Staten Island Advance*

of St. Andrew's Church "in memory of Gen. Hugh Mercer's victory on this spot October 16, 1776."

British Army records show that it was during the winter of 1776–77 that John André, who had recently purchased a captaincy in the 26th Foot, was on duty on the Island. "A gentlemanly and agreeable companion," he was said to have been by a young lady of the DeGroot family, in whose house he was billeted. This house, now known as the Cruser-Pelton house, still stands on Richmond Terrace at the foot of Pelton Avenue. Tradition has it that Prince William Henry, then a young midshipman in the Royal Navy was also billeted there briefly.

André's name is associated with other Island houses: the Post house on the North Shore, said to have been originally a De Hart farm, often used by British and Hessian commanders as headquarters for raids across the Kills. André, who got along well with the Hessians because of his ability to speak German, was said to have used the house as a command post and so agreeable was he to the young people of the area that family tradition, as late as the 1920s, kept this pleasant impression of him. The Inn at Richmondtown, now part of the Restoration village, also has an André association in the frequently repeated story that, while staying in the Inn, he wrote his will: a will that disposed of an estate, in the opinion of James Thomas Flexner, author of *The Traitor and The Spy*, that in modern currency would total close to half a million dollars.

Another successful American attack was launched against the British redoubts on Richmond Hill early in August, 1777. This time St. Andrew's suffered considerable damage to its windows when British troops fled into the church and Americans drove them out by pouring in rounds of musketry.

Two weeks later, General John Sullivan—who had carried Lord Howe's message to the Continental Congress the previous year and had later been exchanged—headed another

attack with about 1,500 men who slipped across the water late
in the night of August 21, 1777. The troops, separated into
two detachments, moved rapidly about the North and West
Shores early the next day, inflicting considerable damage on
the enemy whose numbers had been lessened considerably
when Howe embarked most of his army on July 23 and
sailed off to capture Philadelphia. There were, however, still
five regiments of British, Anspachers and Waldeckers at the
Watering Place and the German Lieutenant General, Baron
Wilhelm von Knyphausen, was in command.

Military experts have questioned the wisdom in Sullivan's
separating his forces and sending them in a series of attacks
over the Island on the twenty-second, but, in his opinion, he
had won a victory with thirty-five tons of hay and a barn
burned at Decker's Ferry, six regiments put to rout, and
between four hundred and five hundred of the enemy killed,
wounded or captured. American casualties were about 150.
British claims of a considerable number of Americans killed
and three hundred prisoners taken were at variance with
Sullivan's report of victory. Lieutenant Colonel Christopher
Billopp had distinguished himself with his command that day,
but the friends of the Dongan family were saddened by the
news that young Edward Vaughan Dongan, commander of
the Loyalist 3rd Battalion of New Jersey Volunteers—a collateral descendant of the famous Governor Thomas Dongan,
the son of Walter Dongan—had died from wounds received
in the fighting at Blazing Star along the shore. The *New York
Gazette and Weekly Mercury* noted that he left "a young
distressed Widow . . . Their only Child died a few hours before him."

Often there were other than military raids from both sides
across the Kills and Sound. British troops went over in search
of cattle and sheep to take back to supplement the nearly
depleted herds and flocks of Island farms. There were "cow-

boys" from Jersey who also came across with twenty or thirty head of cattle to sell to such Tories as Judge Ryers, who grew rich in acting as purveyor to the British. The story was told that often these cowboys reversed procedures by stealing back the cattle and then reselling them to the Tories, who bought the beeves again either knowingly or unknowingly.

While there was often an exchange of prisoners for a variety of reasons after the smoke of battle had cleared, both armies were aware of the advantage to be gained by capturing a certain officer for a certain reason. Americans across the Sound at Amboy and the Kills in Elizabethtown were adept as were the British at this game.

Captain Nathaniel FitzRandolph of Woodbridge, New Jersey—also known as Randall—was a hero to Jersey and Island patriots for his dash and daring. On June 5, 1778, he added considerably to his reputation by capturing Colonel Billopp. That night, Billopp, along with other King's men, was attending a ball at the Disosway's house in Blazing Star. The Disosways were avowed Tories, but secretely they were aiding the American cause at every opportunity. Mrs. Disosway was FitzRandolph's sister. Knowing about the ball, Fitz-Randolph made his plans to capture Billopp after he left the affair. During the evening—so the story goes—the daring captain came over by whaleboat with about fifteen of his men who quietly seized the guard about the Disosways' house. Making certain that his quarry was inside, FitzRandolph waited patiently till Billopp came out, mounted his horse and rode off.

Rivington's New York Gazette continued the story: "We are informed, that the party which surprized Christopher Billopp, Esq., at Staten Island, carried him to Woodbridge in Jersey, where he remained until an order was sent thither to remove him to Morris-Town, where it is said he is confined in gaol. Mr. Fitzrandolph, of Woodbridge, conducted the enterprize, and treated him very kindly. Mr. FitzRandolph had some time before been enlarged from his parole upon an exchange of prisoners."

Later the Governor wrote to General Washington "on the subject of the exchange of Prisoners taken on Staten Island by Capt. Fitz Randolph." The Jersey legislature soon after ordered "a genteel sword to be presented to Captain Nathaniel Fitz Randolph, of Woodbridge, in consideration of his merit and services."

The daring captain continued his successful forays over the Island but finally he, too, was captured and for a year and four months endured the cruelties of a British prison in New York. His exchange was "arranged" through the efforts of several of his men led by Peter Latourette, who purposefully captured Captain Abraham Jones of the British army so as to effect the exchange.

Learning that the captain was ill in the tavern at Decker's Ferry, Latourette and three or four others went over to the Island. Since they were not in uniform they moved about easily. Nor did the guard at the tavern suspect anything as they playfully wrestled outside. As soon as the guard had stacked arms for supper, the Woodbridge men took over. The captain, his mouth stuffed with a handkerchief to muffle his cries, was spirited out to a boat and was quickly rowed over to Bergen Point and an American outpost, where he was kept till FitzRandolph was exchanged.

But the valiant FitzRandolph's days were numbered. Less than a month later he was dead from wounds received during an encounter with the enemy near Elizabethtown, part of a force of six thousand troops that had crossed over from the Island in an attempt to push their way to Springfield.

In his report to the commander, Major General Greene wrote on June 24, 1780: "On Wednesday sennight died, that Patriot and terror to the abettors of tyranny, Captain Nathaniel Fitzrandolph . . ."

The *New York Gazette and Weekly Mercury* carried the item: "Nathaniel Fitz Randolph, a noted Partizan in the Rebel

Service died a few Days ago of the Wounds he received at Springfield some Days since in a Skirmish with the British Troops." The gallant captain's cousin, Asher, upheld the family name by continuing to lead raids against the enemy, using whaleboats large enough to carry off the prisoners seized from Staten Island.

Christopher Billopp was obviously rated a desirable prisoner to use for an exchange. Americans at Amboy watched and waited patiently in hopes of capturing him again. From their vantage lookout in St. Peter's steeple they finally saw him on the grounds of the old Manor House on Wednesday, June 23, 1779. There was no moon that night and in the enveloping darkness four or five men, led by David Coddington, Fitz-Randolph's brother-in-law, rowed silently across with muffled oars. It was said that they got the countersign from a black woman but apparently they moved so quietly that they were in the house without arousing anyone. The Colonel was in bed, according to Coddington's story which differed considerably from the one appearing later in *Rivington's Royal Gazette*, which stated that Billopp and his family had been abused and that there had even been an attempt to bayonet his wife and children. "Not satisfied with adding these insults to their distress, tho' Mr. Billopp was unarmed and made not the least resistance, they kicked him before them to the boat, and wounded him with bayonets, behaving in every respect like a parcel of inhuman savages."

The Colonel was taken to Burlington jail where, in retaliation for FitzRandolph's brutal treatment by the British, he was put in chains and given only bread and water. There he was kept until the day after Christmas when he was exchanged for an American officer of equal rank.

The winter of 1779–80 was known as "the hard winter." The Kills and Sound were frozen so thick that at times men and guns could cross with ease. Ice in the Bay also brought easy access to Long Island and New York after the British found it impossible in near-zero temperatures to keep a channel open for boats.

Lord Stirling, eager to take advantage of the new approach over the ice, planned a surprise attack on the main body of British troops at the Watering Place. Stirling was no stranger to the Island terrain, though even as he planned the attack it was buried under masses of snow. He could lay claim to the fact that, nearly four years before, troops under his command had caused the first blood of the war to be spilled on the Island when they had picked off crewmen from the *Savage* filling their casks at the Watering Place.

Despite the intense cold and deep snow 2,500 American troops crossed over safely before daybreak on the fifteenth of January. While certain early historians wrote that Stirling's target was General Skinner's brigade, snug in redoubts near the Cove in the present Richmond Terrace and Bement and Pelton Avenues area, Stirling himself reported that his goal was the Watering Place; but "the enemy having received previous intelligence of our movements, a surprise was out of the question, and as their works were well situated and appeared otherwise strong an assault was deemed inadvisable. . . ." Since his men were suffering from frostbite and there was the danger of attack from British reinforcements from New York, he ordered a retreat.

The detachment that Stirling had sent to Decker's Ferry found that most of the enemy stationed there had escaped; nevertheless, there was a sharp exchange of musketry around the six-sided Dutch Church that the British used as a stable and it was badly burned. Decker's house and eight or nine small boats tied up at the dock also went up in flames. Possibly this was the cause of the great smoke on the northeast shore of Staten Island reported by the British lookout on Manhattan, who also reported that the flag near the Narrows was up, signaling "something."

Newspaper accounts stated that the "Rebels went off Staten

Island yesterday morning with 300 slays loaded with plunder
—Salted Provisions, clothing, blankets and household Furniture. . . ."

Stirling reported that while his troops were on the Island
a number of Jersey marauders followed in their wake and
plundered the inhabitants in "the most shameful and merciless
manner." The soldiers took little plunder and what was taken
was returned to the owners. Much of the loot of the marauders was seized on Stirling's orders and returned. "A very in-
considerable part, indeed, of the troops dishonored themselves
by participating in these enormities," Stirling informed Washington at Morristown.

The return of these troops to Jersey on January 16 ended
any further large troop movements against the Island by
the American Army. But commando-type raids continued
for the remainder of the War.

The previous summer there had been rumors that the
French—now allies—were planning to sweep the British off
Long Island. Later, word came through that Lafayette was
preparing for an attack against Staten Island. Early in July,
1778, certain Islanders claimed that they had seen the French
fleet off Sandy Hook at the same time British wagon trains,
battered from the recent fighting at Monmouth, were loading
aboard ships to move them to New York. That spring, Sir
Henry Clinton had succeeded Howe as commander of all
British forces in America.

There was frequent shuffling of troops to and from the
Island. Transports brought in new units and troops, such as
the Queen's Rangers and the Volunteers of Ireland, who were
moved to other fighting areas in the south or even to the West
Indies where English and French squadrons were manoeuvring. With France an ally of the United States since 1778, the
fighting started at Lexington and Concord had become a
major conflict, with England and France, the main partici-

pants, prepared to engage in battle wherever their forces met.

The Island had no civil government during the British occupation. Christopher Billopp, as head of the Island militia,
was as near as anyone to being in charge of Island affairs since
he had been appointed Superintendent of Staten Island with a
salary of 350 pounds currency. What his brother, Thomas,
thought of all these Tory activities has not been recorded
for Thomas had dropped the Billopp name—wishing to be
called Farmar—when he became a partisan for liberty.

A fleet of twenty-three sail, including victualers and transports conveyed by His Majesty's ships *Albemarle*, twenty-
eight guns, and *Pandora*, twenty-four guns, arrived in the
Lower Bay on November 11, 1782. The twenty-four-year-old
captain of the *Albemarle* was Horatio Nelson. Two days
later, after anchoring off the Island, he went aboard the *Bar-
fleur*, commanded by Admiral Hood, second in command of
the North American fleet. As he came aboard, Nelson found
Prince William—then a seventeen-year-old midshipman—on
the deck watch. This first meeting of a future admiral and
a future king grew into a friendship so close that five years
later the Prince acted as best man when Nelson married Mrs.
Nisbet in the West Indies. While Island records provide no
information as to whether or not Nelson went ashore before
the *Abemarle* left the harbor, it is likely that he did, and it's
more than likely that she sailed away with all her casks filled
from the nearby Watering Place.

Hostile encounters were nearly over. News that, at last,
British and American negotiators had signed provisional
articles for a peace treaty had sifted to the Island by the end
of November, 1782. Loyalist families now realized the urgent
need for preparing to leave their homes and seek a new life
elsewhere in the King's lands. Soon they were drawing up
claims for losses and petitioning for land grants, many of them
in Nova Scotia. The Billopp and Seamen families led the
loyalists leaving the Island, most of them forever.

The Redcoats Go

The last soldier of the King was out of the city by one o'clock on the afternoon of Tuesday, November 25, 1783; a date long celebrated as "Evacuation Day" and still observed by patriotic societies in the city.

Staten Islanders watching the line of British transports sailing down the Bay and out to sea that afternoon knew that their own Evacuation Day wouldn't come for another week. Sir Guy Carleton, the last commander of British forces, was still aboard the *Ceres*, anchored off the Watering Place, and there were a few troops remaining nearby.

The evacuation had been a tremendous operation, hampered and complicated since early summer by the need to transport more than twelve thousand loyalists clamoring for passage to Canada and other British possessions so as to escape possible vengeance from their former neighbors.

Undoubtedly, as many Islanders as could watched the ships sailing away that November afternoon. A description by an eyewitness of the departure, printed in 1877 in John J. Clute's *Annals of Staten Island*, gives rise to the thought that, because of the intervening ninety-four years, Mr. Clute was citing a story told or written many years before by "the eyewitness" rather than that he himself had heard it directly from the individual. Unfortunately, there is no identifying source, but that does not detract from the interest.

The ships sailed through the Narrows silently; the only sound made was the rattling of the cordage in the riggings. "We stood," Clute repeated, "on the heights at the Narrows, and looked down upon the decks of their ships as they passed; we were very boisterous in our demonstrations of joy; we shouted, we clapped our hands, we waved our hats, we sprang into the air, and some few, who had brought muskets with them, fired a *feu-de-joie;* a few others in the exuberance of their gladness, indulged in gestures, which though very expressive, were neither polite nor judicious. The British could not look upon the scene without making some demonstration of resentment. A large seventy-four, as she was passing, fired a shot which struck the bank a few feet beneath the spot upon which we were standing. If we had had a cannon, we would have returned it, but as we had none, we ran away as fast as we could. A few rods from us stood another group, composed of men and women, who gazed silently, and some tearfully, upon the passing ships, for some of the females had lovers, and some husbands on board of them, who were leaving them behind, never, probably, to see them again. It was long after dark when the last ship passed through the Narrows."

On the first of December, Carleton, aboard the *Ceres,* informed General Washington in New York that, wind and weather permitting, he would be embarking with the remainder of the troops and would "take our final departure on the 4th instant."

That day, also, was to be one of farewell and departure for the Commander in Chief. In the Long Room of Fraunces' Tavern in New York he said good-bye to the officers of the Continental Army, many of whom had served with him since that day in 1775 when he took command at Cambridge.

"With a heart full of love and gratitude, I now take leave of you," the General said. "I most devoutly wish that your later days may be as prosperous and happy as your former ones have been glorious and honorable."

The scene, as described by Major Benjamin Tallmadge, Washington's Chief of Intelligence, was one of sorrow and weeping: "The simple thought that we were then about to part from the man who had conducted us through a long and bloody war, and under whose conduct the glory and independence of our country had been achieved, and that we should see his face no more in this world, seemed to me utterly insupportable. . . ."

Six miles across the Bay, from Island hilltops, possibly there were those with spyglasses who saw the barge that carried the great man from Whitehall Ferry across to the Jersey shore. Certainly, Islanders were watching every movement in the harbor throughout the day from every vantage point; nothing that went on about the Watering Place or aboard the frigates *Cyclops* and *Ceres* escaped them. In a few more hours the last of the hated redcoats would climb into one of the waiting frigates and then, in a burst of delirious joy and thanksgiving, the Islanders could start celebrating their freedom.

Staten Island had the dubious distinction of being the last area to be evacuated by the King's forces. It had been occupied longer than any other section of the country and it was the last place to receive a shot fired from one of His Majesty's guns. The last soldier left from the same landing dock where the first invading troops had come ashore seven years and five months before. When the Stars and Stripes were run up on the staff at the Narrows for the first time on the fifth of December, Islanders could joyously shout that the only flag now flying in New York Harbor was the flag of the United States of America.

Soon they had bonfires blazing into the sky all over the Island and there was hearty drinking to a glorious future in every tavern. At long last the terrors and depredations of the war were over. No longer need householders bar their doors and windows at nightfall or tremble at the sound of galloping horses or the crackle of gunfire. No more would their houses and barns be broken into or their horses and livestock be driven off. The poultry was safe, at last, from thieving Hessians and women need not fear that their silver buckles would be torn from their shoes or their husbands run through by some drunken officer's sword.

Martial law had been the Island's only law for nearly seven and a half years. Patriots who had fled across the water to Jersey could soon return. Their houses were in ruins, their fields laid waste, but they could come home. Devastation was on every side. Great areas of forest timber had been cut for fuel. The only church to escape fire and gun damage was the Moravian house of worship on the Richmond Road at New Dorp. The Court House was in ruins. There was little livestock or poultry left and the harvest had been meager. Many of the Island's blacks had been captured by marauders from Jersey and sold again. It was said that there were less than a dozen free blacks left on the Island when the war ended. Rugged days loomed ahead with winter now upon the Island. But Islanders were free, happy in the belief that henceforth, God willing, they would prosper and their lives and their children's lives and those of generations to come would be forever free.

PART 3

The Pattern Changes

Being an island, the water barrier of the Bay and Kills kept most of the Staten Island inhabitants from outside influences and made them "different" to some degree from people living on Long Island or in Jersey. For nearly two centuries after De Vries, the Patroon, had established his first little settlement near the Watering Place, life on the Island—with the exception of the war years of British and Hessian occupation and the threat of invasion from the sea in 1812—had been devoted mainly to farming, fishing, and raising large families.

The first real change came when Daniel D. Tompkins bought a major portion of the Duxbury Glebe from the Episcopal Church of St. Andrew to add to adjoining acreage he'd previously acquired. By 1815 the village that he had laid out above the Watering Place was flourishing. Properly named "Tompkinsville," it was almost on the site of De Vries' first settlement and not far from the quarantine station of the government.

Daniel D. Tompkins, Governor of New York during the War of 1812 and Vice President of the United States under James Monroe, played an important role in the early life of his country, his influence on Staten Islanders was of such importance that its effect can still be felt. For it was Tompkins, more than any other individual, who originally set in motion the Island's change from a rural area of scattered farms, with a population of less than six thousand, to an urban area of great potentiality for pleasant living and prosperous industry and businesses.

Tompkins, along with his village, was involved locally in laying out streets and roads. The most important one was the Richmond Turnpike, which eventually went in a fairly straight line from Tompkinsville, up steep grades for more than three miles, then down to the old Manor Road, along to Willowbrook and Bull's Head, and finally ended at the wharf at New Blazing Star (now Travis). Here, travelers crossed precariously by scow and resumed their journey to Philadelphia over dusty Jersey roads. As part of the promotion for the new venture, the Governor's turnpike was advertised as a stage route considerably shorter and faster from New York to Philadelphia. He was also involved in steamboats and franchises and owned the famous *Nautilus* that plied between the new ferry house at the foot of Whitehall Street in lower Manhattan to his landing at Tompkinsville.

Tompkins was elected Vice President of the United States under Monroe in 1817 and he resigned the governorship. The great and near great now came in even larger numbers to the Island to be entertained in his villa-type country house on old Fort Hill, northwest of the village, with its magnificent view of the harbor. Some of the Hessian earthworks and fortifications were still there, adding further interest. Probably Tompkins' most famous visitor was General LaFayette, who came to the Island for a brief stay in 1824 while making his farewell journey to the country for which he had fought so gallantly nearly a half century before.

The next year Tompkins died, a broken man, cast aside by the Virginia junta that controlled the Democrats nationally, leaving his financial affairs in a sorry condition.

People of importance had first come to the Island as visitors of the Vice President. Presently they came because they were attracted to the area that was being turned into country estates that stretched from the Fort at the Narrows northward along the green hills and curving shoreline. They found on the Island the attractions of a foreign country without the disadvantages of wearisome travel. Many, on discovering the Island's beauty were enchanted, and with the prospect of living there comfortably, especially in the summer, free from New York's heat and the fear of epidemics. The trip across the Bay was an added delight; five steam ferryboats crossed regularly during the day from the Whitehall slip to the Tompkinsville landing. Most ferry passengers found the harbor traffic exciting: brigs and schooners arriving from foreign ports, navy frigates and gunboats in for overhauling, coastwise barks and brigantines heavy with cargo, and little fishing boats, piraguas and other craft darting in and out among the ships at anchor. And if a passenger needed further stimulation there was always the ferryboat barroom for all kinds of food and drink.

The most pretentious house erected by 1821 was the "Marble House" built for the Vice President's daughter, Arrietta, who was married to Gilbert Livingston Thompson, a young naval engineer. The house was square and imposing, of "marble" (limestone) brought from Kingsbridge, near the Spuyten Duyvil, where there was a well-known quarry. The mansion was surrounded by gardens of exotic shrubs and flowers and the outbuildings, including the stables and coach houses, were larger than the houses of most native Islanders. The view, noted one writer, commanded "as magnificent a panorama as ever greeted the eye, continually enlivened by passing sails and steamers." Today, Curtis High School occupies the site of the Island's first very elegant mansion.

In the decade following, more and more houses and gardens were completed. Tompkins' holdings on the hill, then known as Castleton Heights and later as Grymes Hill, after a series of sales and divisions by various owners, were dotted with villas that were placed so that their occupants could delight in the unsurpassed views of the harbor for miles in every direction.

Another area that was proving fashionable and attractive wound beyond Tompkinsville west to the Kill van Kull "extending around the left shoulder of the Island and well up into the hills." The owner and developer of this choice situation was Thomas E. Davis, a newcomer who had named his holdings "New Brighton" after the English seacoast resort made fashionable and famous by the Prince Regent and his circle. Davis' residence, sparked by the current popularity of Greek Revival, set the architectural style for his development.

With grandiose plans for also having the most elaborate and fashionable hotel in the country set in the environs of his projected village of New Brighton, by 1834, Davis had added wings on either side of his Greek temple, each larger than the original structure, placed a dome over the center, with a two-hundred-foot colonnade along the front. This was the Pavilion Hotel, known at home and abroad in its heyday as the most elegant hotel in the country.

While the greater portion of the Island's native population, now over six thousand, appeared pleased with the influx of newcomers who were buying up large areas, building enormous houses, and driving about in elegant carriages drawn by high-stepping matched horses, there were some who looked on such potential neighbors with a jaundiced eye, especially if the "forners" tried to meddle in politics.

"We don't want any forners coming in here," one exclaimed.

Fortunately for those few Islanders who feared an invasion of their rights, most of the strangers "stuck themselves against the hillside at New Brighton." A few preferred Tompkinsville and "Quorten" (Quarantine) and the new village called Stapleton on the shore toward the Fort, established by William J. Staples and Minthorne Tompkins, the Vice President's son, on land acquired in 1833 from the Vanderbilt family.

Staten Islanders at this time were described as "constituting one of the most peculiar classes of independent yeomanry to be found in the United States."

Their farms were small, usually about forty acres, but highly cultivated and with orchards of fruit trees of many varieties. Their houses, a goodly portion built by Dutch, English and French Huguenot settlers in the previous century and still occupied by their descendants, were neat and white-washed, often of stone. Most of the inhabitants resorted to farming and fishing for their livelihood. Others raised cattle for the New York market.

Woods and fields, occasionally intersected by winding roads, provided, it was said, some of the "most delightful drives, extensive water prospects, and varied rural landscapes to be found in any part of the country. . . ."

A future of increasing elegance for Staten Island beckoned, with tremendous "castles" of wood and stone, and houses of every architectural style springing up among the hills and along the shore as far south as Colonel Billopp's old Manor of Bentley; mansions inspired by Napoleon III's Second Empire, with mansard roofs and heavy towers; Gothic Revival cottages, their steep roofs, eaves, and cornices adorned with wooden lace, while others proudly displayed their Moorish or Egyptian origin.

From Sails to Steam

The first Staten Islander to be rated a millionaire was Cornelius VanDerbilt, one of the most fabulous men ever to climb to great power in this country; a tycoon who, at his death in 1877, at the age of eighty-three, had amassed the largest fortune in America. A descendant of a Dutch family that came across the water from Brooklyn in 1715 to farm their first one hundred acres at New Dorp, "Corneel" (as he was called) started on the spiraling way to fame and fortune at the age of sixteen when he earned one hundred dollars to buy a piragua for transporting passengers and farm produce across the Bay to Manhattan.

Although he was not the founder of the Staten Island ferries, as some present-day writers claim, Corneel's first little piragua was his initial step toward an empire of ships and railroads that topped all others in the country. Piraguas—sometimes spelled periaguas, pettiaugers or periaugers—used in New Netherland, were described by some authorities as having been developed by early settlers from the flat-bottomed scows that plied canals throughout Holland. However, Island historians Charles W. Leng and William T. Davis have stated that the piragua "derived its name and its conception from the Indian 'pirogue'" which the French in Canada adapted from the Indian way of fastening two canoes together for greater stability. Regardless of their origin, piraguas were work boats. They were clumsy, wallowing craft, with high freeboards and a shallow draft that gave boatmen easy access into marshlands rimming part of the harbor's shore. Cockpits were undecked and cattle, firewood, swine, hay, chickens, grain, cabbages and any other farm produce that the owner wanted to ferry were carried along with the passengers. A four-sided lug sail was raised and lowered on a short sturdy mast and was kept aloft by a gaff spar. Since the rudder was attached to an unusually long tiller any strong and nimble boatman could handle a piragua alone, even though, it was said, she'd yaw when tacked, scarcely making leeway.

Big and strong, teenager Corneel VanDerbilt (who always signed his name with a capital D), had no difficulty in managing his boat alone. He was the son, grandson and great-grandson of Staten Island boatmen and farmers, a line of men who had fine farms and added to their income frequently by carrying passengers and freight about the harbor. As to farming, contemporary accounts stress the fact that Corneel hated farming. He worked in the fields only because his father demanded such labor, and it was a way of getting money to buy a boat.

By the time he was nineteen, young VanDerbilt owned the *Dread*, the largest piragua sailing from the Island, and he owned shares in other boats plying the harbor, moving passengers and freight not only from Staten Island but from Manhattan and Brooklyn and across to Jersey. His brightly painted *Dread*, sixty-two feet long and nearly half as wide, with two masts and two lug sails, was the pride of the local piragua fleet and Corneel was known as the Island's best boatman. Because of his reputation, it was Corneel VanDerbilt that the commander of Fort Richmond, on the Staten Island side of the Narrows, selected to carry emissaries to New York with the news that the British squadron blockading the harbor had not attempted a run through that strip of water. New Yorkers were in terror that September day in 1813, fearing that the British warships off Sandy Hook would soon attack the city.

Staten Islanders, ever alert to possible enemy attack, kept constant watch on the British ships. When they heard what Corneel had agreed to do, some said he was foolhardy since the Bay was churning that day under winds close to gale force. But he accepted the run, making sure that the officers understood that, for most of the way, they'd be wallowing through waves, drenched constantly with spray. When he finally landed his passengers at Whitehall Slip safely, but wet and shivering, he had added considerably to his reputation as a harbor boatman.

When the war ended in 1815, Corneel acquired a schooner and sailed to Virginia for a load of oysters, although there could be some question as to his choice of a cargo since the oysters off Staten Island were noted for their fine flavor. Soon, with another schooner, the *Charlotte*—named for a sister—he ventured into coastwide trading with his brother-in-law, John DeForest. During the winter months he commanded the *Charlotte*, carrying goods and freight up and down the coast. Summers were spent on his harbor and river boats.

Although it has been recorded that young VanDerbilt had not been impressed in the beginning with the future of steam-boats and the operations of the Fulton-Livingston monopoly, by 1818 he realized his error and began edging into the new world of steamboating, with its excitement and battles, to break the monopoly held by the Fulton and Livingston combine.

Steamboats had begun puffing about New York waters soon after Robert Fulton's successful run in 1807 with the *Clermont*, a boat which he had designed and built for Chancellor Robert R. Livingston, who held a monopoly from the New York state legislature for steamboat navigation in state waters. Without a license from the Monopoly no other steamboat was permitted into waters controlled by New York state, nor could licensed boats be run except between ports designated by the Monopoly. Connecticut and New Jersey boatmen and shippers were infuriated at such unjustifiable control of coastal waters and closed some of their ports to Monopoly steamboats, flouting whenever possible the high-handed operations of the monopolists.

Corneel's first step into the steamboat world—an area about which he knew very little—was a cautious one. His steam-boating career began in 1818 when he accepted an offer to captain one of Thomas Gibbons' boats. Gibbons owned a line that ran steamboats from Elizabethtown to New Brunswick on the Raritan. Because of the Monopoly, Gibbons' passengers traveling to New York had to transfer to sailing ferries at Elizabethtown for the remainder of the trip to Manhattan, a frustrating situation for a man of Gibbons' disposition.

Along with the command of Gibbons' *Bellona,* VanDerbilt also agreed to run the inn in New Brunswick, also owned by Gibbons. The *Bellona* was new and obviously built from plans freely taken from Fulton patents. It didn't require a seer to predict that Gibbons, with his new boat and his new captain, was ready to do battle with the Monopoly and steam straight to New York.

Corneel enjoyed his illegal steaming to the city for several years, thwarting efforts of the authorities to capture him by hiding in a secret compartment in the boat's cabin. So, with his trips across the Bay and his profits from the inn at New Brunswick (run by his wife, with his teenage brother behind the bar), the young captain's financial condition flourished.

Finally the excitement of beating the attempts to arrest him came to an end. After a series of court cases brought against Gibbons reached the United States Supreme Court, Chief Justice John Marshall presiding, handed down the far-

reaching decision that no state had the right of granting exclusive franchises for steamboat lines, such as the one held by
the Monopoly. Free at last to compete legally, the Gibbons'
line could plan a prosperous future.

Such a future also attracted Corneel VanDerbilt. With the
Monopoly's control broken he soon set about establishing his
own steamboat line. By 1829, his Despatch Line was cutting
fares to the discomfort of competitors. Inevitably, he organized other steamboat lines—up the Hudson to Albany, and
through Long Island Sound as far as Providence, where he
became known as the "King of Long Island Sound." A new
vista opened up in 1840—the growing world of railroads—a
career that brought "Commodore" VanDerbilt power and
riches unequaled by any other American of his day.

There were numerous other Islanders who earned their
living on the water by ferrying and by coastal trade and
there were many engaged in oystering. Contemporary newspaper advertisements indicate that horsepower for boats,
rather than steam, was used, particularly the "horse-boat"
that moved passengers and wagons and an occasional carriage
across the Kills from Port Richmond to Bergen Point; a system that had its breath-taking moments since such boats
could be carried downstream with a strong tide unless the
ferryman whipped his horse into a fast pace on a treadmill
aboard, thus operating the boat's side wheels. On shore, small
boys watching the race with horses and tide shrieked and
howled at the sounds of pounding hoofs and cracking whip.
Another horse-boat ferry was used at Blazing Star—now
Rossville—moving passengers and vehicles across to New
Jersey. And, as late as 1828, clumsy piraguas were still wallowing through the Kills and Bay.

The first steam ferry in the world, the New York Hoboken
Steam Ferry, began operating across the Hudson in September, 1811. Six years and two months later, November 29,
1817, to be exact, the 146-ton *Nautilus* made the first steam-
ferry run to Staten Island. Daniel D. Tompkins, Vice Presi-

dent of the United States, had obtained the sole right to operate steamboats to the Island the previous month. The *Nautilus,* operated by the Vice President's Richmond Turnpike Company, was scheduled to be the connecting water link from New York to the Island for the new Richmond Turnpike that promised a shorter and safer postchaise route to Philadelphia.

Records indicate that the *Nautilus* continued to steam back and forth between Whitehall and Tompkinsville on a regular schedule for eight years. Then the 153-ton *Bolivar* was added, followed in 1826 by the 129-ton *Marco Bozzaris,* providing seven round trips daily during the summer. By 1832, the *Nautilus* had been retired, whether for scrap or on some smaller run was not recorded. Regardless of her unknown fate, the *Nautilus* deserves to be remembered. Not only was she the Island's first steamboat ferry but she was also the first "tugboat" ever to operate in the harbor. That second claim to fame was brought to the attention of today's Islanders by journalist Drew Fetherston in an article published in the Staten Island *Advance* on August 25, 1968, captioned: "Granddad of harbor's tugs also doubled as Island ferry."

"We were yesterday delighted," stated the New York *Gazette and General Advertiser* on January 28, 1818, "to see the Nautilus, steamboat, tow up the ship Corsair from the Watering Place against the current in an hour and forty minutes, a distance of eight miles.

"We cannot here omit to suggest the propriety of employing this powerful steamboat to tow up vessels of every description in all cases of calms or light winds, or even when ice is floating up and down the channel.

"We are convinced that both owners and underwriters would find it to their interest to fall upon some plan of securing the services of the Nautilus in all extremeties of the kind here noticed."

In the opinion of Mr. Fetherston: "the Nautilus had assumed its second role quickly." He credited the exhaustive research of Mr. George Swede of Hasbrouck Heights, N.J., for valuable information concerning the history of New York steam tugs for the period covering the initial tow of the *Nautilus* up to 1861.

Ferrying and towing for the next twenty years brought in double revenues for steamboat owners. Since during that period, Cornelius VanDerbilt had acquired a substantial interest in the Island's steam-ferry business, the double revenues from his boats' double operations added further to his mounting fortune; however, following the launching of his *Sylph*, in 1844, towing and ferrying became separate operations. Ferryboat designs were changing and tugs were evolving into powerful craft that could move anything about the harbor. No one could have been affected more than the Staten Island boatmen.

The Clove

The Dutch called it *Het Kloven*. Before long other settlers were calling that sharp cleft in the hills, "the Clove."

The Clove, or cleft, where it begins between Emerson and Grymes Hills at Concord is now softened by the thousands and thousands of tons of earth trucked in to raise the road level for the Staten Island Expressway, the link between the Goethals Bridge to New Jersey and the Verrazano-Narrows Bridge to Bay Ridge in Brooklyn.

Before the coming of white men, Indians used this natural opening between the hills as a link from the north side to the Narrows lookout on the east. Early settlers followed it long before it was surveyed and recorded as a public highway, about 1705. If tradition can be believed, the first house in the Clove was put up about 1690, the site being a mile north of the Richmond Road, which is considered the Island's oldest road. The builder was probably the doughty Captain Cornelius Corson who had acquired sizable grants in 1680. The original house was of native stone, one-and-a-half stories high. Occupied for more than a century and a half by descendants of Captain Corson, during those years it had been enlarged to three times its original size.

British army engineers' maps indicate three structures along the Clove Road when His Majesty's troops took over the Island in the early part of July, 1776. Perhaps those engineers were unaware that one of the buildings shown on their map was the home of Daniel Corson, a grandson of Captain Cornelius. However, the British commander, Sir William Howe, soon knew that there was such an Islander. For, Daniel, in the excitement of hearing the Declaration of Independence read at the Rose and Crown—which the General was using as his headquarters—whether from overimbibing or from a combination of both, had been indiscreet enough to say loudly that he'd rather have one commission signed by the American George Washington than a dozen signed by King George. A treasonable utterance, and doubly so with the Island under British control. Daniel's friends started him homeward as soon as they could.

A few days later, Daniel had a visit from Sir William and his staff. An aide alighted to see if the General and the others could have some dinner. But Mrs. Corson was busy making butter and asked to be permitted to finish churning before serving the officers.

"I'll make the butter," said Sir William, "while you make the dinner."

Apparently dinner and butter were ready at the same time and, according to the story, the General and his officers enjoyed the food.

On leaving, Howe asked his host's name and, on hearing that it was Daniel Corson, quickly said: "Why, you are the fellow who made that treasonable remark about your King."

The punishment could have been severe but apparently Mrs. Corson's cooking had put the General in a good mood. He mounted and looking down on the Corsons, said: "I see you're about to have an addition to your family. If it's a boy, name him for me and we'll forget what you have said."

In due time the child was born, a boy. The Corsens attended the Dutch Church on the North Side and there all Corson babies had been christened. But the new baby was taken to the Church of St. Andrew at Richmondtown and there, on February 25, 1777, was christened William Howe Corson. Daniel and his wife had done what they had promised, but they continued to do everything they could to aid the army of General George Washington.

It is interesting to find in the records that Daniel's son, Richard, took title to the farm in 1804. At his death, in 1823, he left to his "beloved wife Margaret my lower dwelling room and upper bedroom together with the use of my Garret, Entry, cellars and Kitchen and as much of the Household and Kitchen furniture as she sees proper to retain for her own private use. . . ."

In addition she received "my riding chair, my best horse, two of my best Milche cows and keeping for the same . . . also one fourth part of the Poultry, and the privilege of getting as much firewood and fruit on that part of my Farm herein after devised to my son Cornelius, as she shall want for her own private use only; together with the use of one half of my Garden . . . I do also give to my wife my colored woman named Phillis."

Richard also gave his wife his silver and the interest on all his monies, bonds and notes. She continued to live in the old house and even after she sold the farm in 1830, to John King Vanderbilt, she remained in possession of the rooms willed to her by her husband. The Negro woman, Phillis, and several others who had been slaves but who were now free stayed on with the old lady until her death in 1848.

By the 1840s, a number of elaborate houses set among well-kept gardens had been built in the Clove and on its surrounding hills. It was a community composed almost exclusively of Vanderbilts or their connections. Midway up the hill to the east, forming the entrance to the Clove at Concord, stood the Italianate villa erected by Commodore Cornelius Vanderbilt's nephew, Charles M. Simonson. This house still looks down on Concord, although considerably remodeled. About half a mile further along that hill was the large house of the Commodore's youngest brother, Captain Jacob Vanderbilt.

Across the valley into the Little Clove was the square frame house of the VanDuzers. The Commodore's sister, Elinor Jane, was married to Daniel C. VanDuzer. About four hundred feet on the same side of the Little Clove Road was the house of the Haskells, also relations. Overlooking the valley from the west was the towered mansion of the Commodore's daughter, Alitia, who had married L. B. LaBau. This house is now the Swedish Home for the Aged. A large house of another Vanderbilt daughter, Ethelinda, married to Daniel B. Allen, stood on the eastern slope not far from her Uncle Jacob's. The Allens had bought eight acres from her father's cousin, John King Vanderbilt, who had bought the Corsen holdings. This latter Vanderbilt had put up a white frame house, modest in size in comparison to the others, on Clove Road near the northeast corner of the present Victory Boulevard. It is listed in the *Aia Guide To New York City* brought out through the efforts of the New York Chapter, American Institute of Architects in 1969. Mr. Vanderbilt had remodeled the Corson farmhouse for his stepdaughter and her family by raising the roof of the main section, extending and facing the front story with brick and putting a veranda across the main part of the house. Known as the Corson-Vredenburg house, the structure was razed about 1930 when Beverly Avenue was cut through by a developer who put up rows of small houses.

Along with villas and farmhouses, the Clove of the middle nineteenth century had several Gothic-type cottages. Two of these were erected by the Britton brothers, Henry and Abraham, Jr.; Henry's house was on the east side of Clove Road. Still standing, it is occupied by the John Franzrebs who are noted for their riding academy. Abraham Jr.'s house was occupied into the 1960s when it was razed to make way for a highrise apartment house. Another Gothic cottage is the steep-roofed one at 1336 Clove Road, well past a century in age.

Life in the Clove, from all accounts, was pleasant and leisurely. Everyone had good horses for riding and driving. There were tea parties and dinners, evenings of whist or backgammon or singing around a piano. Skating was fine on Britton's mill pond when the ice was thick enough. There were steep hills for tobogganing and often farm sleds, well-cushioned with straw and drawn by a team of plodding oxen provided fun for groups of young people riding through the snowy valley on a cold moonlit night. For those who preferred faster movement, there was a cutter or a two-seated sleigh or a pung jingling with bells drawn by a fast-trotting horse or pair.

In the spring and early summer, gardens were sweet with the scent of lilacs and lilies of the valley, peonies and the deep red flower of the strawberry shrub. Wisteria and honeysuckle dripped from trellises, roses and pinks brought added delight. In addition to green lawns and flower and vegetable gardens, nearly every place had a smooth or not so smooth croquet ground. Introduced from England prior to the Civil War, it was a favorite game for young and old. Courtships flourished, it was said, when evening croquet, romantically lighted by candles in sconces attached to the wickets, brought longer playing time for devotees. Later, tennis courts were laid out following Miss Outerbridge's introduction of that sport to the Island.

In the spring the blossoming fruit trees throughout the Clove were especially beautiful. Later, there was an abundance of cherries, peaches, plums, pears and apples. Currants, gooseberries, grapes, blackberries and raspberries also provided succulent tasting. For a full quarter of a mile along the west side of Clove Road bordering the Britton property there was a row of cherry trees, some white, others red so deep in color that they were almost black. There were cherry trees about the Britton house, too, and Mrs. Britton, determined to keep the flocks of hungry birds from spoiling the fruit, kept a shotgun handy on the veranda by her chair and fired whenever any feathered marauders appeared.

Abraham Britton owned the mill at the head of the pond which, about 1825, had been formed by damming the Clove brook. His sons had icehouses nearby, where the ponds' harvests were stored. For years the Island's ice industry was headed by the Britton family. Ice harvesting was an important activity in the Clove, just as was iron mining atop Clove Hill and in the Little Clove in the 1850s. The Crystal Water Works, which used the clear water from the myriad of springs throughout the valley (pumping it to the North and East Shores), came later as another commercial activity.

In 1888, the formation of the Richmond County Hunt Club with its club house in the Little Clove between the VanDuzer and Haskell mansions brought the excitement of seeing pink-coated riders on galloping horses following baying hounds intent on running a fox to earth. The fox den was higher up the slope toward Emerson Hill. After the club moved to Dongan Hills, some seven years later, the property was acquired by the John Deere family of Moline, Illinois, which also owned considerable acreage on the west side of Ocean Terrace. This latter land is now the site of the Staten Island Community College.

The first church in the Clove was the first Baptist Church organized on the Island. In 1809, this congregation erected a small building twenty by thirty feet on the west side of Clove Road, a few feet from Richmond Road. From this modest structure came all the other Baptist groups on the Island. The old church was razed in the 1870s. A few of the old gravestones, covered by brush and vines, remained until the construction of the Staten Island Expressway. Amost opposite the Baptist house of worship was St. Simon's-in-the-Clove which had grown from the mission chapel started in the 1850s by St. John's Episcopal Church, Clifton. The brick structure, which had replaced the wooden St. Simon's, was demolished to make way for the Expressway. A handsome, new St. Simon's now stands on Richmond Road, about half a mile from the old church, near the junction with Fingerboard Road.

Two other houses of worship were erected in the Clove: a small white Reformed Church chapel was put up in 1915 on the south side of the present Victory Boulevard, between Clove Road and Grand Avenue, and St. Nicholas Roman Catholic Church, in the 1920s, on Northern Boulevard and LaBau Avenue. Instituted by the Brighton Heights Reformed Church and directed by the New York Classis, church services and a Sunday School were conducted for sixteen years in the Clove Valley Chapel by students from the New Brunswick Theological Seminary. St. Nicholas still ministers to a large congregation.

Unfortunately, in the division of Mrs. Vredenburg's estate in 1889, one of the heirs—at odds with her brothers and sisters because of her unsuitable marriage to a young man half her age—sold her portion of the property to "outsiders."

One of these purchasers put up a large building on the northwest corner of Clove Road and the Turnpike with the intention of running it as a roadhouse. But, since he could never obtain the required consent of the adjoining property owners for a liquor license, the place became a boarding house called Sunnyside. As a way of advertising, the proprietor prevailed upon trolley motormen to shout: "Sunnyside" when they came to the corner. Before long the name began to be used, especially by newcomers to the Island, and through the years the name has stuck, despite the annoyance of those who preferred the old name of the Clove, a name not duplicated elsewhere in the city, This Sunnyside is often a source of confusion for the post office and parcel deliveries since Long Island also has a Sunnyside.

Other descendants of Mrs. Vredenburg acquired parcels of the old farm which had been left to her in 1870 by John

King Vanderbilt. A grandson, John Frederick Smith, bought a portion covering 15 acres at the northeast corner of Clove Road and the old turnpike. This included the Vanderbilt white house. Mr. Smith never lived in this house but rented it to John King Vanderbilt's grandnephew, Joseph Mortimer Vanderbilt who, many years later, became the father of Amy Vanderbilt, the authority on etiquette. In 1895, Mr. Smith, who had already made a fine reputation in the Island world of real estate, insurance and banking, built a small house on the corner of his property. This house remains in his family.

The first real estate development in the Clove was started by the Clovena Company in the area bounded by Clove and Little Clove Roads and the Turnpike. A sale of building lots was held May 4, 1901, with Cornelius G. Kolff, auctioneer. Streets named Oswego, Seneca, Tioga, Oneida, Schoharie, Niagara and Genesee had been laid out and the inducements of cement sidewalks, macadam roads, city water, gas and electric lights were emphasized as part of the promotion.

The second real estate venture was pushed in 1906 by Wood, Harmon and Company in the development of a tract along the eastern side of Clove Road and the south side of the Turnpike. It was called South New York, with avenues named Grand, Glenwood, Van Cortlandt and Alpine. The fifth was renamed Dudley in memory of a small boy, Dudley Swartz, who died soon after the section was built upon.

There was a lot of excitement in 1914 when the *Right of Way*, starring William Faversham, was filmed about the Clove Lakes, selected, the movie people said, because of the area's resemblance to the St. Lawrence River.

This area of great beauty, covering close to 200 acres with its chain of four little lakes stretching for more than a mile below wooded hills, was acquired in 1923 by the City of New York for a park. Over the years Clove Lakes Park has evolved into one of the city's finest parks, enjoyed by thousands and thousands of New Yorkers and out-of-towners, who go there by way of the five-cent ferry across the Bay

and then by bus or bikes or afoot. Others come over the
bridges by car or bus. Islanders are more inclined to use their
park during the week, letting the visitors take over on weekends.

Two of the lakes are used for boating and it is obvious that
many of the boaters never before have handled an oar. The
playing fields for football, soccer and baseball are laid out
near Clove Road in an area known fifty or more years ago as
"the Swamp," which was formed by the overflow from abun-
dant springs. The Swamp became popular for skating since
it froze over quickly because of its shallowness and it was safe
for children.

Along with the attraction of playing fields are bridle paths
and trails winding along the lake and up through the woods.
Young fishermen cast their lines into the lakes. Small children
squeal with delight on the swings and slides and splash in the
wading pool. Scores of picnic areas throughout the woods
are in constant demand. There's even a place further up the
hill among the sassafras and elder bushes that small boys solemnly swear was an Indian cave. Indians are far more exciting
to talk about than how the shaft really got there—through
the excavating efforts of a man named Houseman who, soon
after the Revolution, was hunting for gold in the serpentine
rock.

The park also lures thousands of music and drama devotees
whenever the Metropolitan Opera or the Philharmonic or
Shakespeare-in-the-Park comes to Clove Lakes.

The borough office of the Park Department, a handsome
stone building with lines similar to early Island houses, is at
the park's Clove Road entrance. Where the waters of the
first two lakes join under the double arches of a stone bridge
is a building, also of stone, housing a restaurant and a boathouse.

In the opinion of many Islanders, city planners could have
picked a no more inappropriate site for a year-round ice-
skating rink than the one selected along the south end of the

park at Victory Boulevard. The rink was selected, in addition to a stadium in the South Shore, as the Island's World War II memorial. From the beginning of the project there were controversies and delays. Apparently the base of the site had not been thoroughly examined because soon after excavation work commenced it was stopped abruptly so that piling could be pounded into the mire and shifting, bottomless muck below. Costs soared from the original estimate and the completion date was constantly changed. Further target for criticism is the lack of adequate parking for those using the rink.

With the city's Silver Lake Public Golf Course stretching down to the east side of Clove Road, the stables of a riding academy bordering the course and public tennis courts within a mile, this area of the Island offers more sports and outdoor diversions for young and old than any other section. It's also a pleasant area of small homes and gardens. Only two complexes of highrise apartments—and these are nearly a mile apart—have crept in before the rigidity of zoning.

The Clove Valley is a base, too, for students of all ages. Public School 35, officially named the Clove Valley School, trains its pupils for junior high. For several decades the Augustinian Academy, on the hill sloping down to Clove Road at Howard Avenue, has been a Catholic High School for boys. And, in the summer of 1967, the Staten Island Community College, the first community college founded by the Board of Higher Education as part of the City University of New York, moved into its fourteen-million-dollar campus on Ocean Terrace, a 40-acre tract skirting the Staten Island Expressway. This two-year college offers its students either a career program or a transfer program. The latter curriculum covers liberal arts, science, engineering or business. When two buildings are added in 1975 to the present three, the capacity expected will be for 5,300 full-time day students.

The college atmosphere evoked by SICC students is increased by students from Wagner congregated at the shuttle bus stop on Clove Road for transportation to their college on the top of the hill.

The only dark cloud at present looming over the community is the project of widening Clove Road and Victory Boulevard to lessen heavy traffic lines that stretch from the intersection lights during certain peak hours of the morning and evening and on weekends. But, since the widening of Clove Road has been projected since 1911, hopeful inhabitants are praying for *status quo*, so that the century-old maples and black walnut trees will not crash before the thrusts of roaring bulldozers.

Factoryville

Up to 1820 most Staten Islanders had supported themselves and their families by farming, fishing and other kindred pursuits. There was of course a scattering over the Island of shoemakers, tanners, blacksmiths, carpenters, weavers, tailors, tinsmiths and others who met the needs of the inhabitants. On September twenty-fourth of that year, a new opportunity to earn a living was offered when the Island's first industrial enterprise began operations: a dyeing and cleaning establishment set up by some Bostonians and New Englanders in a "spacious and commodious building" on the North Shore near the site of today's Broadway and Richmond Terrace in West Brighton. The latest machinery necessary to carry on dyeing and finishing ("in the best manner") of broadcloths, cashmeres, satins, plush, silk-hair and other materials had been installed and the new company was also prepared to clean garments of every description as well as carpets and blankets and "to remove mildews and stains from cotton and linen goods."

Staten Island had been selected as the base for the operation because it promised to be "the seat of extensive manufacturing establishments" in the future. On the opening day—September 24—guests at the elaborate celebration included such important dignitaries as the Attorney General of the United States, the Secretary of War and the Mayor of New York. Following an inspection tour of the dye and processing building, an elegant dinner—with a dozen or more toasts drunk—was held for the distinguished guests and officials.

The dyehouse of the new enterprise—Barrett, Tileston and Company—was said to have been on a scale "heretofore unknown to this country." The company flourished from the beginning and the Island gained thereby. Skilled dyers and printers arrived from New England with their families, adding to the population. Houses and some of the dyeworks buildings were floated down from Maine in ships and set up along the east side of Broadway for the workmen. As befitting his official rank in the company, Colonel Nathan Barrett leased a large house on the Shore Road, which later became the famous Fountain House, one of the finest hotels on the North Shore and a noted meeting place for the great and near great. There was a convenient waterway in from the Kills so that vessels could float up to the dye building and load and unload cargoes.

Four years from the day the enterprise started operations the company had close to 150 employees engaged in dyeing and printing a variety of fabrics, the colors of which were described "as brilliant and permanent as the same could receive in Europe or elsewhere."

The company name was changed in 1828 from Barrett, Tileston to the New York Dyeing and Printing Establishment. A village, called Factoryville, was spreading around the dye works, although the post office remained "North-Shore." A much needed store did a profitable business in fancy and staple goods, hardware, crockery and edibles of the best quality, and there was a tailor who made garments of every description, in the most fashionable style. The pond, once called Van Buskirk's after the mill run by that individual, was now Factory Pond. Many new houses were being built for those connected with the dye works on streets that were cut through former orchards and farm land belonging to Colonial Governor Thomas Dongan. Barker Street was named for Captain John Barker, a company official, and Trinity Place received that designation from the nearby Trinity Chapel, established early in the 1800s by the Church of St. Andrew in Richmondtown. By 1871 that little chapel had become the Church of the Ascension, occupying a handsome, new edifice of Staten Island "granite," on the original site. Its slender tower and spire soared 115 feet into the sky.

One of the reasons for selecting the area for the dye works had been the ample supply of fine water, so essential to the industry, that came down from the chain of ponds in the Clove Valley, two miles away, by way of Blake's Pond and a "canal." By the 1890s, however, that water supply was inadequate and artesian wells were sunk on the site to answer the pure water need. By that time the company's full name was the Barrett, Nephews Old Staten Island Dyeing Establishment, and its buildings, bleaching grass plots and water supply covered 20 acres. Six hundred men, women and children were on the payroll and operations were carried on through fourteen offices and one thousand agencies from the Atlantic seacoast to the Mississippi River. The company prospered until 1929. Then it was badly affected by the depression. By 1932 all operations had stopped on the Island.

While those connected with the dye works preferred to call the area Factoryville, map makers as late as the 1850s continued to designate it as Castleton, although others used Cityville, and the steamboat landing was called the Castleton Landing. The first official mention of West New Brighton, it was said, was carried in the New York Manual of 1871. The reason for the name was obvious: west of fashionable New Brighton.

It was about this time that an Englishwoman, described as "one of the most gracious and charming personalities," came to the Island with letters of introduction. This was the famous Mrs. Leonowens, even more famous today as "Anna" who was governess to the eighty-one children of the King of Siam.

Mrs. Leonowens moved with her daughter, Avis, into a small house on Richmond Terrace, at the corner of the present Tompkins Place. There she opened a school for little children and it is due to the reminiscences, years later, of one of those young pupils—Mary Otis Gay Willcox—that lovely "Anna's" stay on the Island was recorded.

"Miss Avis was the real teacher," Mrs. Willcox wrote, "though I remember Mrs. Leonowens sitting at a big table in the schoolroom. Here Mrs. Leonowens wrote her books, and also from here she began to go about delivering lectures on Siam and the East . . .

"She was a brunette with waving hair, parted above a pair of brilliant, eager, searching eyes, rather a tanned skin, and a warm-hearted, affectionate manner which endeared her to all who met her. . . ."

How long Mrs. Leonowens and her daughter lived in the little house on the Terrace wasn't recorded by Mrs. Willcox. But she did say that, when one of the eighty-one former royal Siamese pupils visited New York some years later, Mrs. Leonowens came from Halifax, Nova Scotia (where she was then living), to attend a large reception honoring the Siamese visitors, and that old Staten Island friends and pupils of the famous governess also attended.

For over a century, in fact until the 1920s, Islanders were attracted to the mile-long stretch of the old Shore Road from the Port Richmond boundary at Bodine's Creek, or causeway, to the present Elm Street. This was an important and thriving shopping center. Businesses and services of every kind lined both sides of the thoroughfare although a few, handsome, well-kept residences still remained from the pre-Civil War period. In the beginning the shops were operating in small frame buildings but presently brick buildings of two and three stories were erected.

All needs could be met by scores of enterprises: food,

clothing, shoes, millinery, hardware, jewelry, plumbing supplies, hay and feed for livestock, coal and wood, saloons, a
bank, a building loan and savings association, professional
offices of doctors, dentists and lawyers. The undertaking establishment of John Steers, opened in 1842, occupied an im-
pressive three-storied brick building. There were two churches
and three cemeteries. Livery stables provided horses and carriages for every occasion and the clang of blacksmiths' ham-
mers and the acrid smell of fitting a red-hot shoe to the hoof
of a tethered horse were all part of the daily scene.

Islanders came to deposit money in the Richmond County
Savings Bank or to arrange for a loan to buy a house at the
Staten Island Building Loan and Savings Association, the
second oldest in the state. There were several real estate and
insurance agencies carrying on business; by 1906, the Richmond Insurance Company of New York—organized into a
stock company from the old Richmond County Mutual Fire
Insurance—was carrying on business throughout the country
and Canada from its home office in the towered building at
1621 Richmond Terrace. Next door was the Richmond
County Savings Bank, which had outgrown its first office
close to Broadway. Across the street was the Island's largest
and most popular department store, "Tompkins, the Store
that Satisfies," an outgrowth of a tiny haberdashery opened
in 1877 by seventeen-year-old Frank W. Tompkins.

In the next block was the police station, and next to that
the headquarters of the C. W. Hunt Company, rated the
largest industrial establishment on the Island. Its plants occupied several acres of buildings on both sides of Van Street
and along the waterfront of the Kill van Kull. Charles W.
Hunt was famous as an inventor and pioneer in the mechanical
handling of bulk materials and by 1900 his company had
become the world's largest and leading manufacturer of coal-
handling machinery.

The Church of the Ascension, its slender steeple a landmark for miles around, often attracted worshippers from

Bergen Point, who crossed the Kills in skiffs to attend services. The graves of Islanders who had served in wars predating the Revolution were carefully kept among family plots of the old Fountain and Staten Island Cemeteries adjoining the church to the south and west. The highest ranking officer to be interred there was Brigadier General Alfred Napoleon Duffié of the Union Army whose wife had been Mary Ann Pelton. While on the Island, the Duffiés lived in the old Pelton house at the Cove.

Trolley cars provided the greater portion of transportation along Richmond Terrace, which sounded more elegant and fashionable than "Shore Road." Later, there was another trolley line that started from the brewery near Four Corners and bobbed its way down Manor Road to Columbia Street (now a section of Clove Road) to Castleton Avenue and so to a terminus at the foot of Broadway on the Terrace.

Following World War I, the importance of the North Shore along this portion of the Terrace began shifting as a business and shopping center. In 1921, the Richmond Insurance Company and the Richmond County Savings Bank moved into handsome, new buildings on the south side of Castleton Avenue at Taylor Street. A few years later Tompkins Department Store erected a large building on Castleton Avenue and the southwest corner at Taylor Street. Mr. Grimshaw's popular ice cream parlor on the curve near Broadway closed. Physicians, dentists, lawyers, real estate and insurance agencies moved their office into other parts of the Island. And, by 1930, the Church of the Ascension had moved its place of worship into the former Van Clief mansion on Manor Road, with the intention of erecting a new edifice on that site as soon as funds were available. The old church building was deconsecrated and for a number of years the old parish house was used by the Police Athletic League.

The old buildings remaining were razed eventually or boarded up, unpainted, run-down. Some are used today for storage warehouses or for engineering, fuel oil or heavy machinery operations. The old cemeteries have been vandalised and desecrated, with stones overturned and smashed, skeletons unearthed, weeds and saplings taking over. It is a sad, sad area; doubly sad for those Islanders who remember what once was there. Today, only a few well-kept houses and buildings remain along that stretch of the old Shore Road from Jewett Avenue to Elm Street. At Broadway, the Edwin Markham Gardens, a project of the New York City Housing Authority, occupy the site where once upon a time stood the little dwellings floated down from Maine for dyeworks employees, the site of the Island's first industrial venture.

Forgotten and unknown as Factoryville (and with the "New" of its 1871 name dropped), this part of West Brighton, once so busy and prosperous, seems destined for a kinder fate than that endured for the past half century.

Livingston and Elegance

Livingston on the North Shore, in the opinion of Virgil Markham, was "the special reserve of the British." The area was only about half a mile square but it was "almost completely given over to British and Scottish families whose menfolk commuted during the week and disported themselves in their own gamesome ways at week ends." The games were, of course, cricket and soccer. Professor Markham's description was apt in the opinion of those who knew Livingston well.

From the period of the 1880s up to World War I, Livingston was also the epitome of elegance, wealth and gracious living. Its Bard Avenue dotted with handsome houses was called "the Fifth Avenue of the Island"; the highest of compliments, as New York's Fifth Avenue at that time was considered the most fashionable residential avenue of the country.

But, before Livingston received its name in 1886, when the railroad came chugging into the North Shore and took over the mansion of Anson Livingston as a station, the area was called Elliottville after the noted eye surgeon, Samuel MacKenzie Elliott, who had bought acreage in 1836 along the present Richmond Terrace and Bard Avenue.

Prior to Dr. Elliott's coming the farm lands of the Crusers,

Crocherons and deGroots sloped down to the Kills and stretched inland for nearly a mile. These farms, in 1668, had been part of Governor Lovelace's plantation.

Within a short time Dr. Elliott had built several gray stone houses of his own design—some of which still remain—and the area became known as Elliottville. Throughout his long life on the Island the doctor built more than thirty houses, all of which he lived in as "a tryout" before renting or selling them. He also built a tiny church on the north side of the present Delafield Place. In it was a barrel organ fitted with the entire music of the Episcopal service. This little church later became St. Mary's Episcopal Church on Castleton and Davis Avenues, architecturally one of the Island's loveliest churches.

As an oculist, Dr. Elliott was considered "a genius in his profession." Patients came from all over the country to be operated on. His method and operating procedure consisted of placing the patient on the floor. He then knelt, put the patient's head between his knees and, without any anaesthetic, performed the most delicate eye surgery.

Some of the most important men of the country came for advice and treatment. James Russell Lowell, Francis George Shaw, Theodore Winthrop, Francis Parkman and others came and stayed with their families. Poets, historians, writers and editors were attracted to the area. George William Curtis, who married the eldest daughter of the Shaws, was of national importance as an author, editor, orator and reformer. For more than forty years he influenced public opinion in conducting "From the Editor's Easy Chair" in *Harper's New Monthly Magazine*. He was also political editor of *Harper's Weekly*. After 1863 he devoted himself to public service. He had championed the antislavery cause and later he was a national leader in promoting civil service reform, woman's suffrage and clean politics. A native New Englander, he seems to have loved Staten Island. "Its landscape," he wrote, "is beautiful and suggestive [for the production of literature],

its neighborhood is historic. Its wooded hills, soft with ver-
dure, slope eastward to the Narrows, through which glides
an endless fleet of seacraft; or to wide silent meadows that
fill the west where the narrow Kill, a winding line of light,
threads the land of Beulah; or toward the busy, humming
people north and northwest, toward marts and factories and
rattling steam roads, toward the great city and the broad
Hudson, or southward they look upon the lower bay, and
far beyond, the airy highlands of the Jersey shore undulating
seaward and sinking to the long line of Sandy Hook blending
with the ocean."

Mr. Curtis gave freely of his time for the betterment of
Staten Island and its people, especially in the fields of education and good government. He led the Republican party on
the Island. He was also a founder and pillar of the Unitarian
Church of the Redeemer and conducted its services frequently
when there was no minister for the congregation. His name
endures today in Curtis High School, Curtis Avenue, Curtis
Court and Curtis Place. His house still stands on the northwest
corner of Bard and Henderson Avenues. It is said that the
curve of Henderson Avenue near the house was caused by
sentiment—to save a magnificent elm from destruction. The
road builders bowed before the Curtis wish and curved the
new avenue around the tree.

Mrs. Curtis' father, Francis George Shaw, author and
philanthropist, was one of the Bostonians who came to the
Island because of Dr. Elliott and stayed. He owned much
of the area on Bard, Davis and Henderson Avenues. His house
on Richmond Terrace at Davis was large and elegant, the
only house that was larger and more elegant was the massive
stone residence of John C. Henderson, Esq. on the north side
of Bard Avenue at Henderson Avenue, which was later extended through the estate.

The Shaws had four daughters and one son. Robert Gould
Shaw, who commanded the first Negro regiment in the Civil
War, was killed leading his troops in a charge at Fort Wagner.

The first daughter became Mrs. Curtis; the second married Robert B. Minturn, an erudite Greek scholar who was said to have produced *The Acharnians* of Aristophanes in the original Greek at New York's Academy of Music. The third Miss Shaw—Josephine—married Colonel Charles Russell Lowell, who was killed early in the Civil War. His charger, "Red Berold," was kept in pasture for many years, ever ready "to fling up his head and prance at the sound of martial music from parades marching along the nearby Shore Road." And the fourth Shaw daughter, Ellen, married General Francis Barlow, the boy general and a hero at Gettysburg.

Mrs. Curtis was a famous horsewoman, one of the founders of the Woman's Club of Staten Island and active for many years on the local school board. She was said to have been of great help to her husband and, when writer's cramp reduced him to using a stub of a pencil, she acquired a typewriter, one of the first on the Island, and typed his essays and articles.

As a young widow, Mrs. Lowell became a pioneer of modern charity organizations. She was a founder of the Charity Organization Society of New York City and wrote on public relief and private charity as well as on industrial arbitration and conciliation. Her influence in these fields was so important that she is listed in current encyclopedias.

In commenting on her daughters, Madam Shaw said that Mrs. Minturn would be of great assistance in any society affair; Mrs. Lowell would direct any charitable affair; and Mrs. Curtis, because of her experience with horses and animals, would be perfect in planning a circus.

Another editor, equal in influence and importance to Mr. Curtis, was Sydney Howard Gay who also made his home in the Elliottville area. Described as "a slight, middle-aged gentleman, Roman nosed, eyes set rather close together, whiskers well groomed," he became managing editor of the New York *Tribune* in April, 1862. He maintained that powerful editorship until June, 1866, and was credited with having kept the *Tribune* a "war paper" in spite of his boss, Horace Greeley.

The Gays lived in a little gabled and battened cottage, designed by Ranleigh, that Dr. Elliott had built on Hayley's lane in 1848. Later it became 99 Davis Avenue, one of the most important addresses on the Island. Here came some of the most famous Americans of their time, particularly such abolitionists as the poet, Whittier, William Lloyd Garrison, Wendell Phillips and Lucretia Mott. The cottage was also used as a station on the underground railway. And it's interesting to find that descendants of one of the families saved by Mr. Gay's efforts are living on Davis Avenue at this time.

Years later, the Gay's daughter, Mary Otis Gay, wrote: "At this time we had no postal service on Staten Island, and everybody had to send to the post office for their mail. The West New Brighton office was kept in Mr. Burgess' drugstore, on Richmond Terrace, opposite Mr. Pine's new store, and every winter afternoon Mr. Curtis would stop for Mr. Gay about 4 o'clock and, accompanied by Poozle, the Gays' pet dog, the two gentlemen would take their constitutional, stopping at the post office on their way. Many old residents of the town can remember tall Mr. Curtis, short Mr. Gay, and the little grey dog, taking their brisk walk, the men settling the affairs of the nation as they went. Mr. Curtis' extreme geniality and his ever ready kindness made him a universal favorite, and the progress of their arguments was often interrupted by his friends and well-wishers who were met on the road."

Sydney Howard Gay can be remembered as one of the Island's illustrious citizens; so were his daughter, Mary Otis Gay and her husband, William G. Willcox.

Mrs. Willcox was active in every important movement for the Island's betterment. To list only a few of her interests: she was chairman of the Staten Island Red Cross Chapter during World War I, headed civic and social welfare projects for many years and was an ardent and effective worker for woman suffrage. Mr. Willcox had been president of the Staten Island Hospital, president of the Staten Island Academy Board of Trustees, had represented the Island on the New York City Board of Education and had served as president of that board. He had been chairman of the board of trustees of Tuskegee Institute in Alabama for many years. In acquiring the Richmond County *Advance* he gave the Island its first daily newspaper.

Politically, Elliottville (later, Livingston) was in the town of Castleton, village of New Brighton, and in the third ward. Visitors found the area "elegant, refined, cultivated and literary." Sailors Snug Harbor was its boundary on the northeast and east, the winding lane that became Castleton Avenue was to the south, the Kill van Kull to the north, and the farm of Daniel Pelton covering 18 acres could be considered the west boundary. Beers Atlas of 1874 shows the names of Delafield, Burlingame, Stewart Brown, Gay, Dr. Carroll, White, Melville, Richard, Minturn and Curtis as property holders on the east side of Davis Avenue. The names of Meigs, Shaw, Rayner and Wyman appear on the west side of the avenue. Bard Avenue had fewer names: Bonner, Delafield, Boyd, Stoddard, Garner, Curtis and Henderson. These were large estates. The Bard and Livingston family houses were on the water side of the Shore Road or Richmond Terrace. The Livingston residence was so close to the Kills it was dubbed "Bleak House."

A path ran from Davis Avenue along the shore to the Cove, where the Staten Island Athletic Club put up its boathouse about 1885. The club also had a field for baseball and other sports. Records indicate that rowing and boat clubs dotted the shore line. Boating was a favorite pastime, especially on moonlit nights which were "charmed with song from boat parties oared along the banks of the Kill van Kull."

H. P. Delafield sold part of his estate to the Staten Island Cricket and Baseball Club in 1885. Within a short time cricket fields and tennis courts were laid out. The name was changed later to the Staten Island Cricket and Tennis Club. The Ladies Club, as the name implies, was formed for ladies. And, although they were interested in playing tennis (even in the early days when a lady wore a bustle when playing), they were also noted for their elegant teas and parties. In the 1920s, the Staten Island Academy used the property for its athletic field. Some years later, New York City took over the Cricket Club property and made it Walker Park, named so to honor the memory of a young Livingston resident, Randolph St. George Walker, Jr., a hero of World War I. Fine tennis matches, which carry on the traditions of the old club, are played on the public courts of Walker Park each season.

Worthy successors of Dr. Elliott in the field of medicine were Dr. William C. Walser and his son, Dr. Carl Walser, and Dr. William Bryan, the latter being active up to the 1930s. Today a number of physicians and surgeons live in the area because of the proximity of St. Vincent's Medical Center.

The Richmond Light, Heat and Power Company bought land along the waterside of Richmond Terrace in 1892. After a series of reorganizations, a power plant was completed in 1897. Shortly after that, the clang of the electric trolley cars replaced the clopping of the horsecars that had provided transportation for nearly thirty years from Port Richmond to Fort Wadsworth.

The upheaval of World War I and its aftermath brought many changes to what had been known as "gracious living." Gone were the large houses staffed with servants; gone were balls, cotillions, receptions and soirees; shining equipages with coachmen and footmen and high-stepping horses remained only in pictures and in memories. World War II wiped out what little had been left. No doubt it was the memory of those former, glamorous days, when she was a charming young lady of the 1880s and 90s attending those parties, that drew Alice Austen, the country's first great woman photographer, back to Livingston and the former residence of the

Edward Bonners, in 1951, to spend the last months of her life. By that time, the vast Victorian house had been changed into a nursing home. Miss Austen's room had been the library; but the ornate paneling and window and doorframes remained, reminders of happier days, an appropriate background for one who had recorded that era in such a fascinating way with her camera.

Today, Livingston is an area of pleasant family life. Most of the inhabitants know little of the elegance of its past. The large estates have long given way to smaller houses with trim lawns and pretty gardens. A few garden apartments have been erected. Some second and third generations of families who came to the Island more than a century ago live there; and writers and artists come as they did in the days of Dr. Elliott and the others to find serenity and beauty.

Ice Harvesting

Before the advent of ice-manufacturing units, ice harvested from Island ponds was an important winter crop. The heart of the local industry was in the Clove Valley with its chain of lakes stretching for more than a mile between the hills, although ice was also harvested commercially from a dozen or more ponds throughout the Island and stored in special houses close-by.

Winter was usually a slack time in local industries and a good season on the ponds, when thermometers stayed below freezing and provided work for hundreds of these unemployed, sometimes until the end of February. Teenagers, too, were eager to earn a dollar a day. There were, of course, Islanders who worked year-round with ice, for there was a wide market for the product and the iceman was always a popular fellow, making his rounds from house to house. Saloons, hotels, restaurants and certain markets were also among his best customers.

Henry Britton, whose father had a gristmill at the head of Britton's Mill Pond in the Clove, ventured into the ice business in 1835. At that time young Henry put up a small icehouse near the mill, wisely placing it so that the heavy cakes of ice could be slid into the house, thus avoiding the labor and cost of hoisting. Henry's business prospered and expanded and his ice wagons made deliveries throughout the North and East Shores for many years.

During the 1860s William E. Bradley put up an icehouse at Silver Lake in which he stored his crops from the lake. Later, the Franzrebs acquired the Bradley holdings, operating there until 1902. There were also ponds near Concord and the present Grasmere, where ice was cut for the market. Records indicate that ice cut from the Factory Pond in 1859 was shipped to New York as well as to cities along the coast. Ice cut from ponds formed in extensive hollows left from iron mining near Meiers Corners was run into a small storage house near the present Coale and Chandler Avenues, west of Westcott Boulevard. Elm Park, Willowbrook, Annadale, Rossville and Tottenville were among other places on the Island where ice was harvested. And larger estates having ponds usually had small icehouses for storing those frozen crops.

In 1897 certain dealers joined in forming the Richmond Ice Company. With a capital of $150,000, and by leasing a chain of ponds, this company controlled the local ice harvesting business. New and larger houses were needed and the new-fledged company put up one on the west side of Martlings Pond and, later, another near the "dike" or juncture of the Upper and Lower Clove Lakes. This latter structure, 100 by 200 feet and 50 feet high, was the largest icehouse on the Island. It cost twelve thousand dollars. Inside it was divided into four "rooms." Each room had a capacity to hold up to 3,000 tons. Depending on the closeness of the stacking, the house could hold 12,000 tons or 1,000,000 cubic feet of ice.

Small boys bent on skating, or showing how far they could skim sticks and stones on the ice, were a bane to those responsible for keeping the ponds clear. The ice had to be clean and every precaution was used to keep it so. By the time the ice got to be seven inches thick, harvesting preparations moved into the last stage. Markers were sharpened, horseshoe calks checked and scrapers readied if there was snow to remove, because snow on ice prevented it from freezing further. It was well known that ice thickened very fast after 8 inches. Often, in a few hours, measuring sticks would show as much as 2- to 6-inch increases.

Eight-inch ice was strong enough to hold a horse. Time could be saved if there was no snow to remove but if the surface had to be cleared before marking, a scraper, drawn by a horse, was sent out, a man leading or riding the horse and a second man handling the scraper. As soon as the pond was cleared, a line was run down the ice for close to 500 feet and immediately grooved with a pike. Another line was grooved at right angles to this line. The next marking was that of a space 8 feet long and 6 feet wide. This was carefully checked for accuracy since it was to be the guide for all markings.

The horse-drawn iron marker was shaped like a plow and had 4- to 6-inch teeth in the plow beam. A guide from one side of the beam to the other kept all marks at equal distance. The guide was set for marking the length of the ice block and for its width. For this operation a man led the horse while another guided the marker. When this had been completed the surface of the pond was laid out in hundreds of oblongs, each measuring 22 by 32 inches.

The next operation, that of cutting deeper into the marked ice, required an experienced plower. Unless a plower knew his job he might find himself suddenly floundering in icy water with his horse and plow if the plow bit in too deeply and loosened a section. Next a "canal" of open water had to be prepared. Down this, rafts of ice—three cakes wide and sometimes as long as 144 cakes—would be floated toward a man standing on a plank over the canal ready to split the raft into three-cake sections as it glided down to him. With a long pole the next man deftly turned each section, sending it to the "bar off" who, with his pronged bar, hit the section neatly into three separate cakes as it slipped under the plank on which he stood. A "barrer" had to be agile and accurate. If he wasn't, the penalty was a plunge headfirst into freezing water.

From the barrer the cake floated along to the final stage where it was hooked with tongs and hoisted onto the runway into the house. Before steam power took over, horses were used in this final operation. The Richmond Ice Company in its last great icehouse used steam power and an endless chain with crossbars that carried the cakes aloft to the level being used. Unless the "feeder" with his long pike nudged the cake safely onto the crossbar, a jam occurred that brought shouts and curses from all hands. Sometimes the endless chain would snap, adding to the excitement.

According to usual practice, the icehouse had been built with a double frame, boarded outside and inside, with sawdust packed in the space between. A space of at least a foot left between the ice and the inside of the building was filled with salt hay, and sawdust and salt hay, cut and brought in from the salt meadows on the West Shore. This was tossed over the thousands of tons of ice inside to prevent the cakes from touching.

Years later, telling how the work was done, old icemen said that, when the day's cutting was finished, markings along the open water were carefully packed with snow to keep water from seeping into the marked lines. Weather completely controlled the work. Everything stopped when the thermometer climbed into a thaw. If snow fell, it had to be removed as soon as possible. If rain followed snow and froze, and scrapers couldn't be used, then holes were chopped in the ice so that the surface could be flooded and frozen to insure smoothness. Ice could not be white; it had to be clear.

Only the regular crew worked on the important jobs at the pond. Only experienced men did the marking, plowing, barring, hooking and stowing. The rest of the jobs were done by men who looked forward to this extra work and pay during the winter. In the years of horsepower a dollar a day was good money. Steam power brought a boost in wages, the minimum going to three dollars a day. During World War I, and the last two years of harvesting at Clove Lake, pay went up to five dollars a day, with experienced barrers, hookers and unhookers at the icehouse door getting considerably more. The work day started at seven in the morning, although the plowman usually had started by lantern light an hour or so before. The men worked through the morning, had an hour for the noon meal and then worked on till six o'clock, with lanterns providing the necessary light. Sometimes, if a storm or thaw threatened, they'd keep on till midnight.

When brewers started installing their own ice-making machines, the local ice industry suffered its first blow. No longer would dealers and consumers be at the mercy of the weather to supply their needs for refrigeration, nor would there be the expense of bringing in ice from upstate, New England or New Jersey's Lake Hopatcong when Staten Island winters were too mild to provide a crop. Soon, artificial ice was being made in several plants on the Island and sold to dealers who rumbled in early in the morning to fill up their wagons for the day's deliveries.

The last ice harvest made at Clove Lake, and probably the last cutting of any size on the Island, was during the severe winter of 1919–1920. In spite of the cold, hundreds flocked in to watch the operation. Some to see it for the first time or to show their children. Others—oldtimers—came to follow, again, the familiar sight of the cakes floating to the bridge, going up the long and high incline and finally sliding along the wooden runway into the opening on the side of the dark monster of a house. From early morning until after the sun had dropped behind Clove Hill they came—on foot, in horse-drawn sleighs with jingling bells, or in cars—down the narrow lane from the foot of the hill on Clove Road, near the present site of a highrise apartment adjoining Clove Lakes Park.

Midmorning, one October day in 1920, flames crackled and shot into the autumn sky. Firemen came racing with equipment but soon the icehouse was nothing but a hissing, glowing mass of embers. Ice harvesting on Staten Island had ended forever.

Was Polly Bodine Really Guilty?

The Island's expressway to the Bayonne Bridge walls off a portion of Richmond Avenue in the area known as Graniteville. Curving down from Morningstar Road into a new street set up for local traffic, this old part of Richmond Avenue is used only by the residents of this quiet 500-foot strip of roadway. Most of the houses were built prior to 1900. Several go back to the 1830s. One of these, now numbered 846–848, was the scene of a double murder that included the crimes of arson and burglary. These crimes brought about trials that are still cited in legal histories. Few Islanders know the story of Mary Housman Bodine, better known as Polly Bodine. Moreover, present-day occupants of the house were unfamiliar with the case when interviewed in 1966 by Drew Fetherston, who was gathering material for a series of four articles which ran in the Staten Island *Advance* during October of that year. However, several collateral descendants of the Housman family, on careful probing, will relate what they know about one of the most sensational crimes of the last century; a crime that shocked the country.

Christmas Day, 1843, was nearly over when two boys saw flames licking out of the kitchen wing of Captain George

Housman's frame house and gave the alarm. Neighbors soon had the fire out. The destruction was not extensive, being mainly confined to the kitchen. No one seemed to be in the house. The captain apparently hadn't been able to get back from his trip to Virginia in time for Christmas, and his wife, Emeline, and the baby were thought to be with her father, who lived a couple of miles away. In poking through the debris two neighbors found evidence that the fire had been deliberately set. A moment later two bodies were uncovered: Mrs. Housman and little Ann Eliza with their skulls battered. Within hours the Island was in an uproar.

Captain Housman's widowed sister, Polly Bodine, had spent Saturday night, December 23, with Emeline, who dreaded being alone in the house with the baby. The next morning Polly went to her parents' house nearby for breakfast with them and her teenage daughter, Eliza Ann. On Christmas day she took the stage to the ferry to go to New York. Her sixteen-year-old son, Albert, worked in the drug store on Canal Street kept by George Waite, who also practiced medicine and dentistry. Gossip whispered that for several months Polly had been an "intimate acquaintance" of Waite.

Described as being pretty, with a pale, oval face framed by dark curls, and with dark, arresting eyes, Polly was in her early thirties at the time of the murders. Her marriage to Andrew Bodine had been bitter and unhappy. When ashore from his coastal schooner, he was known to have beaten her and to have thrown her downstairs. Frequently, she had returned with the two children to the comfort and safety of her father's house in Graniteville. Eventually Bodine had deserted his family and, at the time of the murders, records show he'd been dead for several years.

George Housman sailed into port on the twenty-sixth, unaware of the ghastly news awaiting him. Leaving his schooner tied up at a North River slip, he took the ferry to Staten Island. By a strange trick of fate, his sister, Polly, was on that same ferry, accompanied by a neighbor who had brought her news of the crimes.

After the battered bodies of Emeline and her little daughter had been buried together on Wednesday, the twenty-seventh, in the Housman plot in Hillside Cemetery (less than a fifth of a mile from home), feeling mounted even higher to find their killer. Ugly talk and charges had been spreading about Polly.

There was a meeting on the evening of the thirtieth in nearby Gaylord's Tavern, which resulted in a committee being appointed for further investigation of the crimes. The committee, acting as a coroner's jury, was composed of two prominent Island physicians: Dr. John T. Harrison and Dr. Ephraim Clark, along with Judges Littell and Cropsey, aided by Daniel Crocheron, a merchant, and a Mr. Grant. Two days later, on New Year's Day, 1844, Polly was arrested and taken to the county jail in Richmondtown. Waite, too, was arrested and put in jail.

Most of the evidence against Polly was circumstantial. But the police did have pawn tickets which were for jewelry and silver taken from George Housman's home and the pawnbrokers identified Polly as the one who had pawned the objects. Later, however, the accuracy of such identification was questioned when one of the pawnbrokers became confused and pointed out Polly's daughter as the one who had pawned the items. There was considerable confusion, too, from those who had thought they had seen Polly in different places at different times and from those who said they had seen Mrs. Housman moving about her back door.

Trial was set for the summer of 1844 in the Court of Oyer and Terminer in Richmond County, with County Judge Albert Ward presiding. Lot C. Clark was the district attorney. Polly's family had engaged three Manhattan attorneys, headed by David Graham, for the defense. Brother George was doing his utmost to help Polly. His comment was quoted again and again: "My wife and child are gone. That is past. I can get another wife. I can never get another sister." In fact, there were some Islanders who thought the Housman family wasn't showing enough grief at the loss of Emeline and Ann Eliza.

Although Polly had been indicted for the double murders, arson, burglary and receiving stolen goods, she was only standing trial on the charge of murder of Emeline Housman when court opened on June 23, 1844. Richmondtown, the county seat, was thronging with visitors and special boats were bringing the curious to the Island. News hacks covering the affair were adding to its sensationalism. Islanders had shown little sympathy for the defendant or for Waite, although he remained a somewhat shadowy figure compared to Polly. Prejudice was obvious. But, the jury was finally completed.

The trial lasted ten days, during which time several witnesses changed their original stories. The jury was out for hours but, because of the stubbornness of one of the jurors, no verdict was reached. An attempt to select another Island jury was futile so the trial was transferred to Manhattan.

Meanwhile, Polly had been behind bars for more than fourteen months before her second trial commenced on March 20, 1845, again only for the murder of Emeline. Once more the evidence appeared damning . . . the pawning of Emeline's silver spoons and an incriminating note from Polly to Waite. Testimony for the defense attempted to show that, because of her whereabouts, it would have been impossible for Polly to have murdered her sister-in-law.

The jury spent nearly two and a half days in reaching a verdict. This time there was no hung jury. The verict was: "Guilty." However, the State Supreme Court granted a bill of exceptions, with twenty-seven of the twenty-nine exceptions to the judge's rulings upheld. Polly would be given another trial.

For the third trial, after calling six thousand potential jurors, examining four thousand, and finding only ten who were unbiased enough to serve, the defense demanded a change of venire. This was granted and Newburgh, in Orange County, was selected for the legal battle for Polly's life, in April, 1846.

By that time Polly was probably more talked about than any other female in the country. Certainly no one surpassed her in notoriety. P. T. Barnum had a wax tableau of the crime set up in his museum on Broadway, not far from City Hall, where the curious could see "the Witch of Staten Island," a hideous toothless hag, hacking her relatives to death.

Polly found a measure of sympathy in Newburgh, and her attorneys were hopeful when a jury was sworn in and the trial proceeded without undue drama. In his charge to the jurors the judge directed them to suspect the pawnbrokers' testimony, which gave further reason for hope of a favorable verdict. The jury was not out long. The verdict was: "Not Guilty." *Nolle prosequis* were entered on the indictments for the murder of Ann Eliza, arson, burglary and receiving of stolen goods. Polly was free after almost two and a half years behind bars. She returned to Staten Island immediately. There is no record as to how she was received by her neighbors, but her family cared for her till she was ready to start life again with her children, Albert and Eliza Ann, in a little house in Port Richmond.

Polly Bodine lived for forty-six years after she was declared not guilty. Part of that time she worked as a nurse. She had become gentle and kind. In fact, according to an Island historian: "Polly was so tenderhearted that she couldn't kill a chicken for dinner." In later years when she became an invalid, her son and daughter—neither of whom had ever married—cared for her. Eliza Ann and Albert preferred to live quietly although they never lacked devoted and loyal friends. Captain George Housman married again after some years, bringing his wife, a Virginian, to the Island to live in a new house on Morningstar Road.

The marble stones of Emeline Housman and her little daughter still stand in Hillside Cemetery, close to the passing traffic on the west side of Richmond Avenue in Graniteville. Weathered for over a century and a quarter, the lettering on each monument has worn so that it is hard to read what George Housman so long ago had placed there: "Emeline—She lived beloved and died lamented."

For little Ann Eliza, the father had ordered beneath her name: "As like the bright and morning flower / She lived and vanished in an hour / Grim Death with wide and ruthless sway / Made her his mark, and seized his prey."

Mary Housman Bodine died on July 27, 1892. She was given a proper, religious service, with burial in Fairview Cemetery, situated between Castleton and Meiers Corners on the south side of Richmond Turnpike, now Victory Boulevard. Her grave, to the right of the cemetery vault, was for years an object of interest to the curious.

In quoting the family's knowledge of the dreadful affair, handed down generation to generation, descendants of Polly's brother and sister still repeat that Polly was not guilty of the crimes but that she knew who was and was protecting that individual; that she preferred to stand trial rather than have an even worse scandal explode. Such a statement, of course, leads to wild conjecture and speculation, too wild and incredulous to bear repeating. Was Polly guilty or was she innocent? The answer remains shrouded in those dark crimes of long ago, making it doubtful if anyone will ever know.

Oystering

Oyster beds stretching along Staten Island shores were among its important natural resources. Long before the first Colonists, Indians crossed over regularly from the mainland to satisfy their appetites for the succulent mollusks. Later the Colonists were writing of the "vast oyster banks" which provided "constant fresh victuals" during the winter. In fact, so avid was their taste for oysters that a law had to be passed in 1715, banning the taking of oysters between May first and September first. By 1737, a stronger law was passed because "the oyster Beds lying at and near Richmond County, within this Colony, are wasted and Destroyed by Strangers. . . ."

But Island beds were gradually exhausted in spite of strict laws and it became necessary to plant seed oysters. In the early 1800s the village of Prince's Bay on the South Shore became the center of "seeding." Seeds brought up from "the rocks of Virginia" were carefully placed in oyster plantations that extended for miles along the coast.

Dr. Samuel Akerly, famous as a naturalist, wrote that planting and raising of oysters by the 1840s had become a "lucrative trade." Virginia's oysters weren't considered as good as those grown in the colder waters around New York, so, in the spring, large schooners sailed back and forth to bring in Virginia oysters. These were planted off the South Shore to fatten during the summer. By autumn, when they were raked up, they were large and flavorful for marketing. There were other oystermen who sent out their flat-bottomed rowboats along the Kills and Sound, when the weather permitted in March and April, to rake up spawn clinging to stones and shells. These were taken over to the South Shore for planting in beds off Prince's Bay. Oystermen operating out of Tottenville, Port Richard, Chelsea and Mariners' Harbor thrived on their lucrative operations. At Mariners' Harbor "floats" were used for a few hours to give oysters harvested from the South Shore beds a "drink" of the fresher waters flowing down from the Hackensack and Passaic Rivers, before being taken to the New York market. This operation soon resulted in a petition from Southfield and Westfield oystermen asking for permission for "laying down for refreshment their oysters, which privilege is accorded in Northfield and Castleton."

Records indicated that, by the middle of the 1800s, oystering was the Island's most important industry. Hundreds of seagoing schooners, smaller sailing vessels and rowboats were being used. Investment capital was estimated in the millions and thousands of Islanders benefited from the profits.

But it was not an easy life. Experience and judgement were vital and it was no business for a novice. Often cargoes worth thousands were lost at sea. Disease could spread through and ruin oyster beds. And there was the constant danger from certain large fish, such as drums, intent on sucking out the mollusks by crushing their shells.

"Patience and indomitable perseverance, together with a competent capital at hand, are the only conditions which will not insure success, but render it possible."

Eventually, 9,000 acres of harbor bottom were in use as seed beds. Plots of all sizes were leased from the state and staked. The largest plot was said to have been 400 acres; the smallest, less than an acre. Tongs were used in shoal water and rakes, with handles sometimes as long as thirty-five feet, were needed for deep areas.

Of course there were some oystermen who preferred just to go to Chesapeake Bay waters, rake up its natural oysters, and sell them in the New York wholesale market.

For many years the richest Islanders were oystermen. The degree of their affluence was reflected in their houses. Many of these residences were mansions, with massive columns, spiraling stairways, and intricate wooden or iron embellishments. Captains' Row along the Shore Road from Port Richmond through Mariners' Harbor was a tangible example of fortunes made in oystering. Only two or three of their houses remain today on the North Shore, sad caricatures of their former opulence.

Small boatyards had dotted the waterfront to turn out craft for oystering over the years. But it was not until near the close of the century that a shipyard capable of building ocean-going vessels was in operation. During World Wars I and II the North Shore area had become one of the most important and productive shipbuilding sites in the country.

Along with its native oystermen the Island also had another important group of oystermen: free Negroes from Snow Hill, Maryland. Originally hired by Island captains to come north to help in planting new oyster beds, these free Negroes soon brought in their families and settled at Sandy Ground, south of Rossville. Their detailed and interesting story, "Sandy Ground A Tiny Racial Island," was written by Dr. Minna C. Wilkins and published in the *Historian* of the Staten Island Historical Society in 1943.

While the oystering industry prospered so did the residents of Sandy Ground, many of whom owned their sloops and oyster beds. Some were skilled basket makers and black-smiths, too, and Sandy Ground oak baskets and long-handled rakes and tongs were noted for their quality.

Unfortunately, as early as 1884, there was evidence that Staten Island waters were becoming polluted. At the turn of the century Island oystering was badly hit with harbor pollution and sewage. Later, some typhoid fever cases were traced to local oysters and by 1916 the Department of Health condemned the beds. So the oyster business ended locally. Some years ago a story was printed that grandsons of oysterbedders still poach in the old beds, whenever the weather gets cold. Convinced that oysters always free themselves of germs after three or four days of 41° water, and so are safe and clean, these venturesome descendants of old oystermen are said to go out in the dark of a winter night, intent on fulfilling their longing for fat and juicy bivalves, as tasty and good as any that were tonged and raked up more than a century ago.

The Brew Was Good

The Japanese ambassador to the United States, following a visit to the Island in 1879, ordered 100,000 bottles of Bechtel's beer sent to Japan. A sizable order, but then, the brewery of George Bechtel was the largest on the Island and its lager was famous, having won gold medals and prizes in numerous exhibitions in this country as well as abroad.

Local historians identify 1851 as the year of the Island's first brewery. The Italian patriot and liberator, Giuseppi Garibaldi, and his friend, Antonio Meucci, the inventor, were credited by some with having established the first brewery. Others question this claim, saying that the names of these prominent individuals were used for promoting the venture rather than for their skill in brewing. Garibaldi was on the Island less than two years, returning to Europe in 1853. Meucci stayed on in his little house in Clifton, devoted to improving his "telletrofone."

Hundreds of refugees from the 1848 German political upheavals came to the Island at that time, most of them settling around Stapleton and Clifton.

The village of Stapleton was started as a real estate venture of Minthorne Tompkins, son of the former Governor and

Vice President, and William J. Staples. These men had bought the land, once a farm of the Corsen family, from Commodore Vanderbilt and his brother and sisters in 1833; probably in the settling of their father's estate, since he had died the previous year.

At that time the section, dotted with a few small houses, was known as New Landing. Lots and streets were laid out under Tompkins and Staples and some new houses and a hotel had been completed by the time of an elaborate celebration on the Fourth of July, 1836, when the name Stapleton was formally proclaimed. Soon Stapleton was a thriving village, with scores of homes and such businesses as furniture, hat, and shoe stores, saddlery and harness makers, coal and lumber yards, and groceries and feed stores. By 1859 it boasted six hotels and had attracted many newcomers. Before the century ended Stapleton was the most important village on the East Shore.

Among early newcomers there was a goodly number experienced in making German beer. The Island had a plentiful supply of fine water and caves in the hills rimming Stapleton to the west, once used by Hessian troops, provided cool and safe winter storage. The first venture, soon called the Clifton Brewery, was set up not far from the Vanderbilt ferry landing. After several owners it was acquired by Bachmann, whose brew was soon popular, not only locally but also in the city and New Jersey.

The following year—1852—August Schmidt started a brewery further inland, on Manor Road, south of Four Corners, or, as it was more elegantly named, "Castleton Corners." This was known as the Constanz Brewery for twenty-five years. John Bechtel set up his brewery in 1853, in Stapleton, at the head of Broad Street and the present Van Duzer Street. Some years later his son, George, took over the operation.

Because of the poor condition of village roads, George Bechtel, it was reported, found it necessary to stable his horses in New York City; apparently an annoying affair, since it involved "running a steamboat to and from the Island solely for their conveyance." But when Mr. Bechtel enlarged his brewery and added to the number of buildings, he set up unusual stables for his seventy-two truck horses. This structure was two-storied, of brick and fireproofed, with iron beams and floored with tiles sent from Germany. The troughs and racks were also of iron and a bath and hospital for sick horses were set up in the basement. Mr. Bechtel's offices were described as "handsome, with elegant furnishings and decorations of the Queen Anne period." Probably the greatest object of interest to Islanders was Mr. Bechtel's "commodious Russian bath, laid in cement, with imported white and blue tiles."

A third brewery was established in Stapleton in the 1850s. This was later known as Bischoff's. The fourth for the area didn't come till 1870, when Joseph Rubsam and August Horrmann went into brewing. So successful was this new brewery that six years later, at the Centennial Exhibition in Philadelphia, its beer won a top prize, along with Bachmann and Bechtel. A considerable honor for Island beer to have won three gold medals of the eleven awarded United States breweries at the Centennial.

A brief review of the Island's brewing industry shows that the Constanz Brewery was acquired by Monroe Eckstein in 1875. Rubsam and Horrmann, also known as the Atlantic Brewery, took over Bischoff's on Van Duzer at Young Street, and Bachmann's Clifton Brewery merged with Bechtel's in 1911. Beer gardens and restaurants nearby were successful operations and the hotel at Eckstein's, set in twenty-five acres of lawns and gardens, was popular for years.

The rumble of iron-tired beer trucks (many of them brightly painted, with a canvas top to protect the driver from the weather), the jingle of harness and the clatter and clop of the giant horses' hoofs, hauling supplies to saloons and restaurants began to give way, in 1914, to the snorting of motor trucks making deliveries. But, regardless of the method of transportation, the rattle of bottles and the thud of kegs and barrels continued a familiar sound before bars and saloons all over the Island. From the girth and complexion of most of the drivers they were obviously devoted users of the brews that they delivered.

During the years of prohibition breweries and communities throughout the country were hard hit. Staten Island, with its hundreds of families whose living had depended on the making and selling of beer, was well aware of the situation and tried to meet it. Locally, Rubsam and Horrmann converted to artificial ice manufacture and, for a while, produced cereal beverages. Eckstein's, also called the Manor Brewery, tried other lines and kept going till hit by the depression starting in 1929. Some of its buildings remain, incorporated into a shopping area. The old Bachmann-Bechtel plant was used for a variety of operations till badly damaged by fire in 1931. What portions remain are presently used by a popular restaurateur. The brick bottling plant and office are also in use but not for their original purposes.

Rubsam and Horrmann was remodelled and enlarged after prohibition ended. The company flourished for twenty-one years. Piel Brothers bought control in 1954 and operated the brewery till 1963, then Piel's, in turn, was bought by an Indiana corporation and the Island operation was closed.

Rubsam and Horrmann, which started in 1870, operated for the longest period and was the Island's most successful brewery. Today the buildings seem empty. Occasionally, trucks move in and out. Occasionally there's talk of using the site for public housing and other proposals are made from time to time. Meanwhile, the property extends along Canal Street near Tompkins Avenue; the buildings stand forlorn and blank, waiting for a future that never seems to come.

Prohibition Park

When a group of ardent Prohibitionists, seeking an area in which to set up a temperance resort within easy commuting of New York City, discovered a small farm of less than thirty acres south of Port Richmond on Staten Island, the National Prohibition Camp Ground Association believed that it had found a perfect site at last.

The year was 1887. The leader of the enterprise was the Rev. Dr. William H. Boole, a Methodist minister, encouraged by his wife, Ella A. Boole, a dedicated officer of the Women's Christian Temperance Union, who later held the State, National and World presidencies of that Union. Dr. Boole's associates included Dr. Isaac Funk, a founder of Funk and Wagnalls, publishers, and his brother Benjamin F. Funk; William T. Wardwell, an official of Standard Oil and a Prohibitionist; the Reverend Christopher S. Williams and other prominent clergymen.

The acreage purchased was bounded by Watchogue Road and the present Jewett Avenue, then called Pond Road. Within a few months small lots for tents and summer cottages were laid out and a tent for meetings was set up in a pretty grove. The attendance at those afternoon and evening ses-

sions was always large, even though transportation was by
horse and carriage or by walking. This was easy for Islanders
but for New Yorkers it was quite a venture, involving a ferryboat trip across the Bay, nearly four miles by train along the
North Shore to the Port Richmond station and then hiring a
hack to get to the Park.

From contemporary descriptions, particularly the reminis-
censes of the noted editor and lexicographer, Charles Earle
Funk (son of Benjamin F. and nephew of Dr. Isaac Funk) the
early days of the temperance resort were happy and often
exciting to grownups and youngsters alike. Picnic suppers
were held in the nearby grove between the afternoon and
evening meetings. Audiences had to fight mosquitoes while
listening to the lecturers and, as was later pointed out, the
waving of handkerchiefs and the sounds of clapped hands
weren't always signs and evidence of applause.

By 1891 the mosquitoes were less of a problem in the newly
erected, twin-towered auditorium that had succeeded the
tent, and which seated four thousand. Nearby, the Villa and
the Grove House provided rooms and meals for visitors. And,
by 1892, a little trolley car, bobbing over the single track
laid from the Port Richmond station and along Jewett Avenue
to the Boulevard, was a vast improvement over transportation
provided by horse-drawn hacks.

More and more cottages had succeeded the tents in which
campers had spent the summers of the first couple of years.
And streets had been laid out, graded and named for prominent Prohibitionists such as Wardwell, Fiske, Bidwell, Wool-
ley, Demorest, Waters, Neal Dow and St. John, the last two
being governors of Maine and Kansas, respectively. Five of
the avenues so named honored presidential candidates of the
Prohibition party, one of whom, John Bidwell, received nearly
271,000 votes in the 1892 election.

Progress, as well as prohibition, seemed to have motivated
the association. Park residents were Christians, but they represented nearly every major Protestant Church. The Funk

families were Lutherans. Dr. Daniel S. Gregory, who was managing editor of the Standard Dictionary, was a Presbyterian clergyman; the Reverend Joseph Wright was an Episcopalian; and Dr. James C. Fernald, well known as a grammarian, was a Baptist minister. There also were members of the Society of Friends and Universalists. Travel in winter from the Park to Island churches was difficult so religious services were held in the parlor of the Villa on the Boulevard, with a rotation of Park ministers preaching each Sunday. Mrs. Boole was credited with making their schedule, which soon evolved into an undenominational church, said to be the second such church in the country. By 1895 the structure was completed, named Deems Memorial Chapel, to honor the ministry of the Rev. Charles Force Deems, who had founded the Church of the Strangers, in New York City. The Reverend Charles Rawson Kingsley, a Presbyterian clergyman, was installed as the first minister of Deems, a ministry that continued for forty-five years, during which time the little chapel grew into Immanuel Union Church.

That same year of 1895, the private school started the year before for Park children—with Mr. Kingsley as principal—moved into its own building, erected during the summer on land recently acquired from the Jewett estate. A freshly graded and widened street—College Avenue—had been laid out from Jewett Avenue as a proper entrance to the school, which now was called the Westerleigh Collegiate Institute. A full-time principal, Professor Wilbur Strong, was in charge.

It has been suggested that the school's name had been selected to attract students from outside the Park but no information is available as to why "Westerleigh" was selected. The name soon became popular for the area and gradually replaced "Prohibition Park." A change hastened and aided doubtless by newcomers who, although attracted to the community by its rigid property restrictions and high standards of conduct, didn't relish being the object of witticisms on prohibition.

Along with the Prohibitionists the Park was also noted as being the home of such literary greats as Florence Morse Kingsley, author of thirty-one best sellers. Her first, *Titus, Comrade of the Cross*, sold two million copies, and was translated into nineteen languages. Edwin Markham, the poet, lived on Waters Avenue in the house first used by Edward Jewett Wheeler, editor of *The Literary Digest*. Dr. John H. Kellogg of Battle Creek fame was an early resident and there were scores of bankers, brokers, businessmen and lawyers who came to the Park, it was said, as fast as houses could be built for their families.

Two generations later, there is Amy Vanderbilt, whose books have long passed the two million sale of Mrs. Kingsley's and whose advice on etiquette influences millions of Americans as well as other millions around the world who read her syndicated columns in a variety of languages. Amy grew up in Westerleigh, in her parents' typical Park "cottage" on Maine Avenue. She went to Public School 30 on the Boulevard before going to school in Switzerland and she and her husband, Morton Gill Clark, spent a good bit of time in the family's house during the early years of their marriage.

For many years there were only two commercial activities permitted in the community: a small store selling groceries and candies a block or so below the auditorium, and the plumbing establishment of Mr. Missal on Maine Avenue between Wardwell and Fiske. Today, the only change is in the plumbing shop, which became a grocery-deli prior to World War II. The grocery store, established before World War I on the corner of Jewett and Waters Avenues, and the handsome building of the Westerleigh Savings and Loan Association, are where the only businesses are conducted in the community. There's also a firehouse which adds wailing sirens to the noise of traffic over Jewett Avenue.

Westerleigh today still maintains its prestige and reputation as a good and desirable place to live. The present cost of a lot—and there are but a few left—on which to build a house

would cost more than the entire acreage cost those ardent
Prohibitionists in the late 1880s and early 1890s. And any
house, no matter how small, would cost more than the towered
auditorium, where the silver tones of William Jennings Bryan,
the stentorian voice of Theodore Roosevelt, the exhortations
of General William Booth, founder of the Salvation Army,
and the lectures of explorer Robert E. Peary—destined to
reach the North Pole in 1909—thrilled and inspired thousands
and thousands of listeners.

The grand opening of the auditorium had occurred on the
Fourth of July, 1891, and that evening the enormous fieldstone
fountain was turned on for the first time. Ever after it was
one of the features of the Park for the crowds to wait for
and to watch. The colored lights, mounted in glass-protected
niches, shining through the falling water gave young and old
alike pleasure and excitement comparable, it has been said, to
today's Christmas tree radiance in Rockefeller Plaza. Fire
swept through the auditorium in 1904, destroying it and the
carriage sheds and nearby bowling alleys completely. The
Grove House also was in ashes. Neither was ever rebuilt. A
few years later the Westerleigh Collegiate Institute's building
went up in flames and a professor lost his life. Part of the
building was salvaged later by Mr. Keiber, who had a farm
of several acres along Jewett Avenue. Small parties and dances
were held in "Keiber's Hall" for several years. In the 1920s
Keiber's farm bowed to progress and the lure of real estate
development. Streets were run through the fields where vegetables had grown and houses, smaller and less fancy than
those put up by the Prohibitionists, soon lined Constant Avenue and Keiber and Margaretta Courts.

Tennis is still played on the courts laid out by the Funks
more than three-quarters of a century ago. The old section
of Public School 30 still stands on the site of Grove House,
although the original schoolhouse is overpowered now by the
"new" portion that completes an entire block. The enormous
stone fountain at Fiske Avenue, near the foot of the Boule-

vard, remained on its site into the 1950s when, for safety reasons, it was razed, stone by stone. Undoubtedly there were some watching the destruction who remembered the fountain in its heyday of cascades of pure water for the thirsty: the only proper beverage for visitors to the Park. There must still be scores of Islanders who can recall the forbidden pleasure of climbing up the fountain's sides nearly to the overhang and in darting in and out between its arches over the waterless pool.

Flying squirrels once were among the inhabitants of the Park. No one knew they existed till one day Bertram Cutler, a teenager at the Institute, pointed out a "colony" near the Park's boundary on the south to a couple of his fellow students, who watched in excitement as one of the graceful little brown creatures, "spread out like a miniature bearskin rug, sailed through the air from tree to tree." A half century or so later, one of the "fellows" remembered those squirrels and wondered if Bert, who had had a distinguished career with John D. Rockefeller, Jr., remembered them, too.

Although the boardwalks of Prohibition Park have long since been replaced by cement or concrete and the streets have become "one way" because they were too narrow for easy access by cars, the silver maple saplings, planted so carefully in the beginning by the Prohibitionists, have grown majestic and beautiful.

Most of the original "cottages" remain, the majority spared from "modernizing." The little towers, turrets and balconies signify their age, their dignity and their charm. They mellow and add distinction to a community that is rated one of the nicest on the Island.

Miss Outerbridge Plays Tennis

Staten Islanders, backed by the authoritative *Encyclopaedia Britannica*, are delighted with the fact that it was an Island resident, Mary Ewing Outerbridge, who first brought lawn tennis to the United States.

Miss Outerbridge had spent the winter of 1874 in Bermuda with her family, and it was there that she saw the game played by English officers. Returning home that spring, she brought back the necessary equipment of rackets and balls, a net and a diagram for laying out a court. Her enthusiasm for the new sport fired certain members of the Staten Island Cricket and Baseball Club—especially her brothers—to lay out a court on the Club's grounds. The Club, organized two years previously with thirty members, was using the level area along the waterfront formerly used as the Civil War training ground, Camp Washington. Today, the St. George Ferry House, parking lot and railroad tracks cover the site. By introducing the new game to America, Mary Ewing Outerbridge made the Island the first home of American lawn tennis.

Within a brief period tennis became an elegant and pleasant pastime, particularly in the northeast. Men played in various forms of attire. Ladies in long skirts, wearing elaborate hats, and bolero jackets, patted the ball languidly over the net, while modestly holding down their trailing skirts. They appeared more concerned, it was said, with acquiring gentlemen partners than with the rules of play.

A further distinction came to the Island later, for the first National Lawn Tennis Tournament ever played in the United States opened on the courts of the Staten Island Cricket and Baseball Club on September 1, 1880, and continued to September 6. This tournament was not played under English rules nor was the United States Lawn Tennis Association then organized. *The New York Times* reported that the twenty-three entrants were gentlemen from England, Canada and various parts of the United States. They played for a silver cup presented by the Island club and inscribed, "The Champion Lawn Tennis Player of America."

O. E. Woodhouse, entered from Philadelphia, but a member of the Middlesex Lawn Tennis Club of London, England, was the winner. Frank Leslie's *Illustrated Newspaper* carried a sketch of this first tournament and a detailed account in its September eighteenth issue. Among the hundreds of spectators were several parties of ladies and gentlemen on horseback and others who came in phaetons, drays, dogcarts, and, of special excitement and note, in a "four-in-hand."

Erastus Wiman bought the property used by the Staten Island Cricket and Baseball Club in 1885 and the Club moved its playing fields and courts to Livingston. But baseball continued to be played on the old field. The Metropolitan Baseball Club used it as home grounds. Years later this club became the New York Giants.

There was a change of name of the Cricket and Baseball Club after the move to Livingston; henceforth it was called the Staten Island Cricket and Tennis Club. Over the years fine tennis developed in clubs throughout the Island, with play on clay courts becoming popular. The Clifton Tennis Club was famous for its players and tournaments, as were the Richmond County Country Club, in Dongan Hills, and clubs in Westerleigh, New Dorp, Prince's Bay and Pleasant Plains, to name but a few.

The Island's place in the history of American tennis is acknowledged today in the National Lawn Tennis Hall of Fame and Museum at Newport, Rhode Island. Among these displays are the trophies won in the early 1900s by Helena R. Pouch (Mrs. William Henry Pouch) of Grymes Hill, holder of the ladies' national championship. This athletic accomplishment was amazing to those who knew Mrs. Pouch in later life as the distinguished and stately President General of the National Society of the Daughters of the American Revolution, an office held in the early years of World War II.

Tennis is still played with enthusiasm on the Island. The Country Club and Westerleigh are the last of the private clubs. Hundreds also play each season on the city's courts at Silver Lake and Livingston.

Golf, described as "a compromise between the tediousness of croquet and the hurly-burly of lawn tennis" came to the Island, if legend can be accepted, in 1894. It was on an October afternoon of that year that Islanders were made aware of the ancient game. Two members of the Richmond County Country Club left their clubhouse on the Little Clove Road to try their skill in a nearby cow pasture that the Club hoped to develop into a golf course. Before the afternoon ended, both gentlemen had been arrested for hitting balls across a public roadway and endangering the safety of passersby.

In court the judge reprimanded the men and ordered them never again "to strike a ball while playing the silly game in the future when any vehicles or pedestrians were nearby." In spite of the warning, Club members, when not galloping over the fields in chase of a fox, or following hounds on a drag hunt, soon had a nine-hole course along the Little Clove Road, almost as far as the old Richmond Turnpike. Golf was played in the Little Clove for two or three years. The Club property included a little Gothic cottage used as a clubhouse and, at the rear, properly screened by shrubbery, were stables for members' horses and a kennel for hounds imported from England.

In 1897 the Club leased "Effingham," the old Alexander estate at Dongan Hills. The house, built in the 1840s, was large and handsome and the stables of brick had plenty of stalls.

The first golf links were nine holes, but a few years later a new course of eighteen holes was laid out from Todt Hill Road to the Ridge. Today, this course, noted as one of the oldest in the country, is famous. Richmond County is also famed for being the last private club with golf and tennis in New York City. The Club's insignia—a riding crop with three horseshoes—retains the Club's personality, emphasizing its original purpose for fox hunting and riding to hounds. It is interesting to note that, in the founding of this country club, two members of the Outerbridge family—Eugene H. and Adolphus J.—had an important part.

The links of the Harbor Hill Golf Club provided certain New Brightonites with a convenient course in the early 1900s. This club stretched over the present area within the bounds of Prospect and Lafayette Avenues, with Brighton Avenue to the south. It is remembered as a fair course, with a clubhouse commanding sweeping views of the harbor and verandas where members rested with their wives and families after a strenuous round of play.

Prior to World War II, the Fox Hills Golf Club on Vanderbilt property, at Fox Hills along the present Vanderbilt Avenue, was also a popular and convenient course for Brooklynites as well as Islanders. Matches played there remain in the annals of national golf. Tysen Manor's course in the section of Hylan Boulevard, New Dorp Lane, Mill Road and Tysen's Lane, during the 1920s, is now the site of one of the Island's large shopping centers.

Today, Staten Island has five golf courses: Richmond

County Country Club, Silver Lake, Latourette, South Shore and a nine-hole course at Willowbrook, originally laid out for World War II patients in Halloran Army Hospital; ample evidence that golf, despite its beginning, is not a rich man's game.

The Woods of Arden

Erastus Wiman named the old farm "The Woods of Arden" when he acquired the property in 1886. But the history of the place stretches back to 1685, when Governor Thomas Dongan granted 80 acres on the South Side to Dominie Petrus Tesschenmacker, the Island's first resident minister and, as noted previously, the first dominie of the Reformed Protestant Dutch Church in North America ordained in America.

Over the centuries a dozen individuals have owned this land along the waterside and inland through meadows and woods as far as the present Amboy Road at Eltingville. Two of these owners, Dr. Samuel Akerly and Frederick Law Olmsted, were of national prominence and importance. Samuel Akerly was only eighteen years old when he finished his medical studies at Columbia College in 1804. During the War of 1812, as surgeon of troops on duty at the Narrows forts, he became familiar with Staten Island and later bought the dominie's original acreage, calling it Oakland Farm. For ten years the doctor was superintendent and physician for the New York City Deaf and Dumb Asylum but, along with his profession, natural history held his interest. So great was this interest that he became a founding member and officer of the

New York Lyceum of Natural History. He wrote extensively in this field and a report on Staten Island that he prepared, in 1843, for the New York State Agricultural Society remains a valuable source of information on the population, employment, fisheries, minerals and weather of the Island during that period. Because of his studies and writings, Dr. Akerly has been rated the Island's "first resident naturalist."

Records indicate that Dr. Akerly greatly enlarged the original farmhouse for his place of retirement from the city, adding another story and verandas along three sides, before moving in with his family. A perfect retreat for one determined to write without interruptions since city visitors would have to travel by boat to Rossville on the West Shore and then take a hack for the four-mile ride over rough roads to the house.

The Island's first naturalist died in the summer of 1845. Two and a half years later Oakland Farm was bought for Frederick Law Olmsted, a twenty-five-year-old bachelor interested in new methods of farming. Renamed "Tosomock Farm," the 130 acres had cost the new owner's father twelve thousand dollars. Island maps, as late as 1850, continued to use the old name of Oakland Farm and possibly some Islanders continued with the old name, too. But they were well aware of the new owner's new methods of raising wheat—40 bushels of wheat to an acre—and frequently asked his advice. They also watched with interest when he changed from wheat to fruit raising, especially after the five thousand new nursery saplings from France were planted. Olmsted also planted such trees as Cedars of Lebanon, gingkoes, black walnuts, mulberries and lindens in his first attempt at "landscape architecture."

When he went to England in 1850 and, for the first time, saw in Birkenhead the results achieved by city and park planning his life was changed. This change for Olmsted also injected a tremendous influence in the future planning of cities and parks for modern America. Today his work is still vital, bringing inspiration to and contributing to the health of millions throughout the country. His first important prize was won in 1857, with his colleague, Calvert Vaux, for the design and plan of a large central park in New York City. During his long and distinguished career Olmsted designed eighty parks throughout the country, thirteen college campuses, the grounds in Washington around the National Capitol and hundreds of private estates. He was the first commissioner of Yosemite National Park. But he never forgot his ties to Staten Island. In 1870 he served on the Commission for the Improvement of Staten Island. Unfortunately for the Island and its inhabitants, very few of the "improvements" were ever carried out.

The old farm had a new owner by 1870—Dr. William C. Anderson, who used the good, rich soil for raising vegetables needed in special diets of his patients; however, the doctor didn't live in any of the two or three houses on the original acreage. Nor did Erastus Wiman live there when he became the owner. His "Woods of Arden," wrote a visitor, "were as beautiful as those described by Shakespeare." They were also of easy access over the new owner's railroad. This Canadian-born Islander's impact had already been tremendous. Included in his local accomplishments were the reorganization of the railroad, a consolidation of ferries, with a transit hub at the newly named St. George waterfront area, and the construction of a railroad bridge across the Arthur Kill to Elizabethport in New Jersey.

He was also the first president of the Staten Island Telephone Exchange Company, started the central station for Island electric service, and his power station near Richmond Terrace and South Street later provided lighting for his spectaculars, the *Fall of Babylon* and the *Fall of Rome*, designed to bring thousands to the Island. An amusing fact is told by Mr. Wiman's granddaughter, Mrs. Maurice I. Pitou: that the elephants appearing in these shows, while being driven back and forth to stables in Jersey Street, passed the house of William A. Rogers, a noted cartoonist, and from Rogers' sketches of these passing pachyderms the GOP elephant later emerged as the symbol of the Republican party.

Activities directed by Mr. Wiman at his Woods of Arden were varied. Described as "a day resort for Sunday schools, societies and parties generally" other visitors were delighted with theatrical performances on the beautiful grounds laid out years before by Frederick Law Olmsted and with elaborate dinner parties at the Inn "for the leading social groups on the Island."

Mr. Wiman's career was halted when certain of his business rivals pounced when he became financially embarrassed, and had him "arrested for alleged illegal actions." Many Islanders were shocked at his creditors' action and stoutly defended him. Eventually 13 acres of the Woods of Arden property and the old house were sold. The house was leased for a while to a fishing club, then purchased and used for a family residence. Much of the land was cut up into "Seaside Estates": little houses, little plots of land, a fate for which Staten Island seems destined.

The present *AIA Guide to New York City* lists the old house, where Akerly, Olmsted and others lived so long ago, as 4515 Hylan Boulevard, near Woods of Arden Road. Set back from the road among the trees, it's not easy to find unless one knows this Eltingville area.

PART 4

David and the Irish Cowfrog

David Carlin was a spry little Irishman who never had married. When he went to work, he wore the same clothes, winter and summer: a well-brushed dark suit, a white shirt and black bow tie, high Congress shoes with a mirror-like polish and a black derby carefully placed at a cocky tilt. Gray eyebrows and gray mustache dipped in pleasing symmetry. His eyes were so small and deepset that a long look was needed to see that they were brown and lively. His nose was short and straight and often quivered with excitement, especially when he was reporting on the pre-Christmas activities of Granny Goozenheimer, Santa Claus' grandmother, who paid frequent visits to the barn when David was there alone currying the horses.

To have a friend who had a friend like Granny Goozenheimer set a small boy or girl apart, and David was extra popular and busy in December relaying messages to Mrs. Goozenheimer's distinguished grandson.

David was also on intimate terms with Easter bunnies and with ghosts and witches that flitted among the trees on Halloween.

How old he was no one seemed to know or care. From

his stories he apparently had been a lad during the Civil War, for he had driven a wagon that delivered bread regularly to soldiers at Camp Scott on the Island's East Shore. David knew everyone and everybody knew David. Policemen, street sweepers, bank presidents, trolley motormen, judges, doctors, actors, newsmen. Women obviously liked him, but he managed to remain a bachelor and apparently a determined one. A younger sister, who was widowed, kept house for him. She made him comfortable and she didn't nag: a trait he knew all wives had.

He had a green thumb, handled horses well, danced Irish jigs and reels whenever there was a party and was clever handling fighting cocks. And when that sport was legally banned he added to his reputation by always being able to elude any law enforcement officer.

But probably David's chief claim to remembrance is as a story teller. The exploits of Granny Goozenheimer, the growth of such fabulous vegetables as pumpkins and melons, the Dutchman who breakfasted on four-and-twenty duck eggs, and the history of the Irish cowfrog living in Britton's Pond were among his best. The cowfrog story became so famous that finally a reporter from a New York paper came down to the Island to interview David to get the truth.

The truth about the Irish cowfrog that lived for two years in Britton's Pond in the Clove Valley was that it had been smuggled into this country by a man who worked in the ice house at the pond. It was a rare creature. In fact it was the only cowfrog in America and it was the biggest in the world.

The man had cared for his friend tenderly, taking it down to the pond, keeping it comfortable in shallow water along the sandy bank, feeding it well and covering it up when the nights grew cold.

But the frog wearied of such devotion and one day slipped away. The man, heartbroken, tried in vain to lure the creature back. Apparently the frog hadn't gone far from the pond because it frequently spoke in a bellow that was heard all the way to the Kills, two miles distant. Children who had been very good often saw the frog, because it was never afraid of boys and girls. Some small boys boasted they'd ridden across the pond on the frog's back, but they got whipped for such fibbing.

Although some of the icemen swore that the frog weighed 274 pounds, the man always said that it weighed 150 pounds on the ice house scales. "Why exaggerate?" he asked. "Who ever heard of a frog any heavier?"

And then the cowfrog sickened. Two warts on its back that used to be as big as watermelons grew smaller and smaller and, unless you stood within a quarter of a mile, you couldn't hear its voice.

Finally, a young fellow from the same village in Ireland as the frog decided to help. He had a truck and he borrowed a block and tackle. Then, taking his ten-year-old brother along, he went down to the pond. While he slipped a heavy rope around the creature, the lad patted the frog's back so it wouldn't be frightened.

They hoisted their compatriot onto the truck bedded with straw and salt hay, and drove down to the dock at Tompkinsville, where a ship bound for the old country was loading.

Later came word that the cowfrog had arrived safely, had gained back all the lost weight and was living very contentedly in a pond near Tipperary.

Petticoat Lane

More than two hundred years ago the Dutch on Karle's Neck (now New Springville) laid out a new road eastward over the hill to the King's Highway. This road wound near the two-room dwelling of Hank Vanderveer; but "Schelm Hank," as he was called when spoken of (though not when spoken to), was not disturbed by passersby. For, Islanders soon discovered that it was easier to ride two miles farther westward and use the old Poverty Lane that joined the King's Highway at Cocclestown (Richmondtown) than to pick their way around the stumps and rocks that reared up on stretches of the new road.

Hank's house, half buried in the ground, was partly stone and partly timber. Vines thick as a man's arm twined about its walls and over the roof. Only the door remained clear of climbing tendrils and that was because Hank's respect for the power of evil spirits was even greater than his respect for the Dominie who crossed the Bay once a month to hold religious services for the settlers. And, he had protected himself from supernatural visitations by nailing half a dozen horseshoes around his door.

If he'd worn stockings Hank would have stood six-feet-six.

He was half as broad. Once a year his daughter, Nauchie, who looked after him, trimmed his dirty yellow hair. How he earned a living, tradition doesn't say. His fields were overrun with weeds. His cow was little more than a bundle of bones. His hogs were scrawny and his tiny flock of chickens was always scratching hopefully for tidbits in the filthy dooryard. Occasionally he paddled out into the Sound in a canoe he'd fashioned from a log. Later he could be seen trudging back across the fields, a basketful of dripping shellfish or shad or bass perched on his shoulder.

Nauchie was four inches shorter than her father. She had inherited his bulk as well as his stolid disposition. If she longed for friends, she gave no sign that she did. Only once had she given any evidence of sociability, and that had been a day at cider-making time when little Bornt Symonse was struggling to put a barrel of the stuff onto his cart. For a while Nauchie watched him trying to lift the heavy thing then she elbowed him aside, bent, and without any effort shouldered the barrel. But, before dropping it into the cart, she pulled out the bung, took a long swig and then tilted the barrel while Bornt had a drink.

Perhaps it was the drink or perhaps it was Nauchie's strength that captivated the young Dutchman. Next day, which was Sunday, Bornt went up the new road to the Vanderveers, dressed in his brown breeches and smock. But by that time Nauchie had turned shy, or she'd lost interest—if she'd ever had any for the lad—and she hastened his departure by lunging at him with one of her father's heavy oars. A passerby saw Bornt's retreat and the story lost nothing in the telling.

This episode only convinced the young men of Karle's Neck that Nauchie was as lacking in sentiment as she was in vanity. Nor could anyone accuse her of displaying her physical charms through the medium of dress. However, the neighbors were aware of her preference for one garment of a certain color: a blue petticoat that she wore winter and summer. Whether it was the same petticoat, tradition doesn't say. It might well have been the same outer garment because, as the years went by, it became dingier and dingier. Tradition is definite, however, on the number of Nauchie's petticoats. She wore eleven, never any more, for to have done so would have been, in her opinion, a useless extravagance. To the Dutch of Karle's Neck, Nauchie and the blue petticoat were indivisible.

Finally, death came to Schelm Hank. Nauchie remained in the old house although the place grew more and more dilapidated, nestling lower and lower into the ground each year. Like her house, Nauchie grew old and the blue petticoat also reflected its age.

Death finally claimed Nauchie, too. A farm boy hunting rabbits found her lying under a hedge in the north lot. Neighbors came and arranged for her burial by her father's grave in the fields and the young Dominie from the North Side read the Dutch service.

There is no record of who was responsible for the disposal of Nauchie's few possessions, nor was it known whether or not the faded blue petticoat was interred with her. But if it had been buried with the old woman the garment didn't remain long beneath the ground. Within a week of Nauchie's death, small boys peeking in the open doorway of the old house scampered away in terror when they saw the petticoat moving slowly across the hearth.

At first no one believed their tale. Whoever heard of a petticoat living alone in a house? But when Pieter Tyse, cutting across the fields on a moonlit night, saw the petticoat bobbing ahead of him, few could dispute Pieter's statement for he was such a sober young man. Later, when four young fellows reported seeing the garment fluttering in the light of the firebrands they were carrying as a protection from wolves in the nearby woods, Karle's Neck farmers could no longer scoff at the talk. They solemnly admitted

that the Vanderveer farm and the adjoining roadway were
haunted by old Nauchie's blue petticoat.

For years, particularly in the moonlight, the petticoat was
often seen gliding along the road, moving in and out of the
caved-in house, or just aimlessly bobbing over the fields and
among the trees. Soon the road was being called Petticoat
Lane, a place to avoid when the sun went down. Only a boy
anxious to prove his courage ever ventured near the house
and then only in the safety of bright sunlight.

One hot summer day a tremendous thunderstorm crashed
and rolled across the Island. Trees toppled, and houses and
outbuildings were struck by lightning. A bolt went through
Nauchie's rotted roof and within minutes only a few smol-
dering embers remained.

After the storm several of the neighbors poked carefully
through the charred timbers and ashes. But there was no
sign of the petticoat. Not even a shred of dingy blue could
be seen among the rubble.

Although the petticoat was seen no more, stories about
it began to spread and be told and retold year after year.
And the road along which the garment had bobbed and
fluttered so long continued to be called Petticoat Lane,
in spite of all the efforts of newcomers who wanted to have
it known by the more elegant name of Rockland Avenue.

Watchogue and Other Places

To the uninitiated, Watchogue, on the west side of Staten Island, bears an Indian name similar to that of Patchogue on Long Island. But this is not a fact. Watchogue wasn't named by or for any Indians. It's a contraction or slurring of "Watch Oak."

Two centuries ago that flat and sandy area was called "Merrilltown" for the obvious reason that most everyone within a mile radius bore the name of Merrill. At that time the most prosperous member of the family was Isaac, or Ike, a descendant of Richard Merrill, an English settler, who, for some forgotten reason, had been dubbed "the intrepid." Ike farmed the same acres that had been granted to Richard's son, William, by the English governor. In addition to fine melons, cabbage, beets and other produce that he raised for the city markets, Ike had orchards of apples and pears and a magnificent stand of oaks that stretched for half a mile along the road. Fat cattle grazed in his meadow, reaching to "Beulah Land," the big hummock to the west that sloped down to the salt meadows. Dappled gray farm horses stomped at night in his red stable, along with the carriage horses and "Major," the sleek chestnut pacer that Ike raced each Saturday afternoon in the flats at New Dorp. Inside the stone, story-and-a-half farmhouse, Tabitha, Ike's dutiful wife, brought up four sturdy sons and four pretty daughters.

But such contentment couldn't last when Brunsen moved into Merrilltown. Brunsen helped himself to the best of Ike's melons, plucked the finest russet apples, took the plumpest chickens from the hennery and relieved the cows of milk that should have flowed into the Merrill milk room. Brunsen was a clever fellow: too clever for his neighbors, they soon discovered, especially those who had him brought before the justice of the peace when they caught him making away with certain of their prized possessions. What could you do with a rogue who could write as well with his left hand as he could with his right? Not only could Brunsen write with both hands going at the same time across the paper, but he ate with both hands, he shingled his roof with both hands, he whitewashed his fences with both hands, sloshing the stuff on at the same time. He was, whenever he wanted to be, one man doing the work of two.

But rarely did Brunsen spend his time on such honest activities. Ike muttered and swore whenever he saw his new neighbor. Like the other Merrills, he soon learned that after a visit from Brunsen a dozen pullets, a bushel of russets, a new rake or shoats from the latest litter would be missing. However, when the rascal started helping himself to the straightest, tallest, young oaks, Ike got his gun. Next to his wife and children, even before his horses and hounds, those oaks had his love.

Determined to thwart Brunsen, Ike patrolled his farm from dawn to dusk and throughout the night for the next three months. Guarding those trees became his prime interest, and only when he was forced to take time to eat and nap did he relegate his watch to a farm hand.

To the query of "Where's Father?" or "Where's Ike?" the answer was always: "watching oaks."

Before long, neighbors and passersby were pointing out "Watch Oak Farm" and peering through the trees hoping to see Ike or one of his men on guard. As part of their Sunday afternoon pleasure, Island farmers drove by the Merrill place, advising Ike to watch oaks and deal with Brunsen.

As for Brunsen, no one knew where that ambidextrous rascal finally went. Some chuckled that Ike's buckshot had scared him away; others said he'd crossed the Sound to Carteret. He disappeared that winter as silently as he'd filched his erstwhile neighbors' hens and turnips. Soon he was forgotten, as forgotten as the name of Merrilltown and as forgotten as the reason why Watchogue on Staten Island rhymes with "rogue," while Patchogue on Long Island rhymes with "hog."

To newcomers the name, Bloomfield, is better known than Watchogue, although it's doubtful that the area will ever be noted as a pleasant place in which to live. Bloomfield is now the site of the world's largest above-ground storage tank for liquid natural gas. The monstrous facility, 97 feet high, 62 feet deep and 270 feet in diameter, can supply, it is said, 200 million cubic feet a day to meet New York City's needs. The gas is piped from the Mexican border to the Island, then liquified and stored. Considered "a push-button operation" it can be handled by a crew of from twelve to fifteen men.

Bloomfield and nearby Chelsea on the Arthur Kill, once called Pralltown and Peanutville, are the victims of giant, earth-moving machines that churned and tore up the fields where strawberries and sweet potatoes once grew and where acres and acres of blueberries and clumps of sassafras stretched toward the water. The land has been leveled as part of a 750-acre industrial park from Mariners Harbor to Travis. Nearby, Chesapeake & Ohio, Baltimore & Ohio Railroad facilities and the proximity of the Staten Island Expressway and the West Shore Expressway—the latter sched-

uled for completion by 1972—offer an added incentive
(planners hope) to new Island industries. Another projected
industrial park for the Island will cover 300 acres in Charleston and Tottenville.

Travis, once called Long Neck, New Blazing Star, then
Linoleumville because of the factory operating there for
nearly sixty years, is now the home of two Consolidated
Edison generating plants. The smoke often belching into the
sky from its tall chimneys indicates the plants' 845,000 kilo-
watts of generating capacity; an accomplishment not ap-
preciated particularly by homeowners in the area.

Southward across the marshlands from Travis lies the
world's largest garbage dump—"sanitary landfill" in the language of city officialdom. By whatever designation, the fact
causes considerable anguish to Staten Islanders. Nor does the
city's plan for a mammoth eighty-million dollar incinerator
to burn more than 30 percent of the city's daily garbage
collections, along with the "development" of a new dump-
ing area north of Travis into Bloomfield's River Road, rouse
any enthusiasm.

One area here that seems to have some measure of security
from the thrust of garbage, landfill and industrial progress
is the William T. Davis Wildlife Refuge. Honoring the
memory of the Island's noted naturalist and the country's
foremost authority on cicadas, its 260 acres owned by the
city lie between Signs Road on the north, Victory Boulevard on the west, Richmond Avenue on the east, and, on the
south, Main and New Springville Creeks.

Originally intended as a sanctuary for birds and other
wildlife, it has, over the years, introduced nature to children
from the greater metropolitan area and taught conservation
to thousands. The Staten Island Institute of Arts and Sciences in its *Proceedings* of September, 1961, stresses: "For
the present and future the Refuge might be defined as the
inner core of the land area and the surrounding areas might
provide developmental and environmental studies of varying

effects on a natural area by encroaching urbanization . . .
therefore the importance of this project transcends local—
ie, county and state—application and may be, instead, of
national importance."

Politics and Problems

Flames crackled and shot into the summer night and inhabitants of nearby Tompkinsville ran into the streets to watch as building after building in the Quarantine Grounds was gutted. A group of thirty prominent Islanders watched soberly as the volunteer firemen's pumper and hose cart, bells clanging, were pulled in but those who had set the fires that night of September 1, 1858, knew that the hose was already slashed and unusable.

By right of eminent domain, New York State—despite strong local protests—in 1799 had taken for a lazaretto or pesthouse, 30 acres of land, part of the 340-acre Duxbury Glebe owned by the Church of St. Andrew. Hospital buildings had been erected over the years for the care of yellow fever and smallpox patients, and others with contagious diseases arriving in the Harbor. The Quarantine staff wasn't restricted to the high brick walls surrounding the hospital grounds, the boundaries of which in present day designations were Hyatt Street, St. Marks Place, Victory Boulevard and the waterfront. They moved freely about Tompkinsville and carried fatal infections to hundreds of Islanders for fifty-eight years. Petitions and strong protests had been

made by succeeding generations of Islanders but state officialdom took little action.

The September night was warm and windless when certain well-known citizens met beneath a tree on Fort Hill
before setting out on their mission. Each man carried a
bundle of straw, a container of highly flammable camphene
and a supply of matches. Arriving at the unscalable high
brick wall, they found handled beams awaiting them on the
ground, which they put to immediate use as battering rams.

According to the record there were only three yellow
fever patients in the hospital. These men were carried out
carefully and placed in an open shed, where, it was noted,
they enjoyed the fiery affair. Furnishings from all buildings
were removed, including a cat and a canary, before a match
was struck. No one was injured during the night, nor were
there casualties hours later, when the remaining buildings
were burned.

The Island was put under martial law with the arrival of
the Eighth Regiment. Newspapers spread the story throughout the country of riots and arsonists, labeling Islanders:
"barbarians, savages, incarnate fiends, sepoys." Actually
there had been no rioting. Arson had been knowingly committed by men of courage and integrity to rid the Island of
a grave health menace. They gladly interpreted the resolu-
tion passed by the Board of Health of the Town of Castleton that citizens should "abate without delay" the insuffer-
able nuisance at Quarantine.

As leaders, John C. Thompson and Ray Tompkins, the
latter a grandson of the former Vice President of the United
States and Governor of New York, were taken before
County Judge Henry B. Metcalfe. They were acquitted.
However, Islanders did have to pay for the damage estimated at $133,822, which was raised by the issuance of
bonds by county supervisors.

There was no attempt to rebuild Quarantine. *The Florence Nightingale* was converted into a floating hospital and

anchored in the Lower Bay to meet the need. Finally two artificial islands—Swinbourne and Hoffman—were created a safe distance off South Beach and hospitals to care for contagious patients were built there.

The ugliness of riot appeared on the Island during the Civil War, spilling over from the draft riots on Manhattan which started on July 13, 1863. For three days, whites in the city (especially those of Irish background), who hated the Negroes, believing them the reason for the war and rivals for jobs, murdered and tortured blacks, literally tearing some apart and kicking others to death. Not until troops from the recent great battle at Gettysburg were brought home did the city rioting, looting, shooting and burning stop.

On the Island mobs moved over the Shore Road between New Brighton and Factoryville. Shouts and the steady tramp of feet on the plank walk, clearly heard in the hot July night, were terrifying sounds to families of "Black Republicans" who finally fled for safety to the homes of friends inland. Islanders on horseback and in wagons and carriages saved exhausted blacks, running in panic from the mobs. On the East Shore thirty guns were taken from the Tompkins Lyceum and the Staten Island Railroad barn was burned, as were the homes of several Negroes. Port Richmond residents defended their handsome little village by putting a cannon at the bridge crossing Bodine's Creek.

For three centuries roads have been a major problem and source of strife and argument on the Island. Richmond County, before the consolidation of Greater New York, was comprised of five towns: Castleton, Northfield, Southfield, Westfield and Middleton. Serious planners were well aware that not one of these towns was a large enough unit to have control of road building and improvement, but for nearly two centuries that was the law even though three miles of driving could take one over portions of the roads of these five towns. And five different kinds of construction would be used in that distance. Widths that varied from 12 to 16 feet. Macadam surfaces that varied in depth from 4 to 8 inches. Obviously, Island roads and construction had evolved into a crazy quilt pattern. Finally a county road law was enacted which did bring improvement and uniformity.

When Staten Island, as the Borough of Richmond became part of New York City in 1896 and the first Borough president, George Cromwell, a Republican, took office on the first of January, 1898, one of his major responsibilities was the direction of building and maintaining Island highways. This particular procedure was followed until 1963 when a new city charter took highway authority away from each of the five borough presidents of the city. Highways are now part of the centralization of city government and the mayor's office is in control; a situation that causes many Islanders considerable anguish and inconvenience.

Planning for the Island's future frequently becomes a political conflict between the City Planning Commission, the borough president, the mayor's office and irate individuals. Along with heated controversies over roads and placing of parkways and expressways is the tremendous problem created by the city's use of topographical maps prepared in 1907–12. These maps show, among other things, locations of water courses but very few identifying landmarks still exist to pinpoint a building lot, thus the properties of hundreds of new homeowners are frequently flooded and ponded.

Heavy truck traffic along the North and East Shores makes highway extensions necessary and controversies flare as to where these extension routes of the Shore Front Drive should be placed. Rumors have it that the Shore Front Drive along the South Shore—a favorite project of Robert Moses —will be scrapped since it's no longer favored by city officialdom, although state planners have given no indication of their lack of interest.

But the greatest battle between Islanders and official planners rages over Richmond Parkway. Projected more than two decades ago when Mr. Moses was commissioner, it would cut through the Island's "Green Belt," the city's "last miniwilderness"; an act of vandalism and desecration of nature, in the opinion of thousands, equal to running a six-lane expressway through Manhattan's Central Park. Here six hundred acres of trees, flora, wildlife, glacial ponds and long views of the Lower Bay, Raritan Bay and the Kills to the west stretch across nearly five miles of the Island's ridge of serpentine hills: an area unsurpassed for future hiking, horseback riding, fishing, boating, picnicking and relaxation. A 20-mile hikers' path to be called Olmsted Trailway, honoring Frederick Law Olmsted, is being projected there by the Sierra Club, the Staten Island Green Belt Natural Areas League, and other organizations. The Green Belt runs through the present Latourette Golf Course and Park, High Rock Nature Conservation Center, Pouch Boy Scout Camp and Henry J. Kaufmann Campgrounds of the Federation of Jewish Philanthropies. High Rock was originally used as a Girl Scout Camp but later was sold to developers for a large sum by the Girl Scout Council of Greater New York. Before bulldozers smashed through its hills of oak and hickory a roused group of conservationists prevailed upon the city to save the land for a nature conservation center.

The original Richmond Parkway routed through the Green Belt has been the subject of legal proceedings and court actions for years, with conservationists versus the previous city administration, the borough president, the Staten Island Chamber of Commerce, the Tri-State Transportation Commission, New York State Transportation Department and the United States Bureau of Public Roads: the latter because the Federal government is paying one-half of the parkway cost. Alternate routes have been proposed. The sixth and last, as a compromise route to skirt the Green Belt area, was brought forth after conferences that ended in February, 1970, with the Chamber of Commerce, the Director of Staten Island Development and later with the governor, the lieutenant governor, the attorney general, the mayor and the United States Bureau of Public Roads.

Shortly afterward, legal action to enjoin the city and state from adopting alternate Route Six was brought against the State Transportation Department by the Staten Island Citizens Planning Committee, the Staten Island Green Belt Natural Area League and two groups across the Bay: the Municipal Art Society of New York and the Green Belt Emergency Conference.

Is the Green Belt destined to be saved? Thousands of nature lovers fight and pray that it will.

Islanders to Remember

"Who are the Staten Islanders who made the strongest impact upon Staten Island in the first fifty years of the century?"

The Staten Island *Advance* asked this question early in 1950 in its search for "the first ten" of the first half of the twentieth century. These notables were selected by the local newspaper, assisted by an "advisory board" of Islanders, each of whom had been asked to nominate ten individuals.

"The First Ten" were announced on April 29, 1950, and they included civil leaders, office holders, clergymen, businessmen and philanthropists. Of special interest was the fact that two women were included with their husbands, thus actually increasing the number to twelve. The explanation given: "Each woman made a tremendous impact in her own right; however, in each case the woman who was selected first worked with her husband as a partner, then continued on after his death."

Alphabetically, the names were:

Ellsworth B. Buck, former congressman, former president of New York City's Board of Education, a founder and officer of the Staten Island Community Chest, also a founder and officer of the Staten Island Zoological Society. Active and an officer in the Chamber of Commerce and on the boards of the Boy Scouts, Staten Island Hospital, Staten Island Academy and a long list of other local organizations, Mr. Buck, with others, interested Mayor La Guardia in setting up the Staten Island Free Port in Stapleton.

George Cromwell as first Borough President—1898-1913 —"guided the first steps which changed the Island from a community of isolated villages into the compact entity we have today." Mr. Cromwell also served the Island in the Assembly and as a state senator.

William T. Davis "through his genius, work and gifts probably contributed more than any other man to the cultural life of Staten Island in the last fifty years—and his influence will be felt for generations to come". The Staten Island Museum is his chief memorial.

Dr. and Mrs. Louis A. Dreyfus gave Hero Park to the city as a memorial to the Island's World War I dead. The vast sums that the Dreyfuses gave so generously to Island hospitals, health agencies, schools and colleges, to name but a few, came from Dr. Dreyfus' skills as a chemist in improving the method of making chewing gum and artificial rubber. He also invented a cold-water paint.

Cornelius A. Hall was the first candidate for borough president to be nominated by both Democrats and Republicans. High among his achievements for his borough were the rebuilding of the St. George ferry terminal, destroyed by fire in June, 1946, the transfer to the city of the Island's poor bus system and the establishing of the Island's road system when he was Commissioner of Borough Works.

The Reverend Pascal Harrower, rector of the Church of the Ascension, West Brighton, for forty-four years (for eighteen years its rector emeritus), and a canon of the Cathedral of St. John the Divine, was the "dean" of the Island's Protestant clergy. He gave leadership to the entire community and was the first to hold nondenominational com-

munity services. "A distinguished churchman, his degree of
tolerance and faith in humanity drew together the religious
groups of the Island into greater bonds of brotherhood and
understanding."

Cornelius G. Kolff, "Staten Island's most obedient servant," was in almost every civic movement in the Island's
first fifty years as the Borough of Richmond. As a realtor
Mr. Kolff was responsible for negotiating many important
land purchases, among them the East Shore city piers and
World War I Fox Hills Base Hospital. In 1895 Mr. Kolff
had played an important part in forming the Staten Island
Chamber of Commerce. For a quarter of a century he
served as its secretary and had held the presidency for three
years. As chairman of the Chamber's Free Port committee
he had a vital part in bringing the foreign trade zone to the
Island.

Samuel I. Newhouse as publisher of the *Advance* was,
perhaps, "the greatest single force in the last quarter-cen-
tury in uniting Staten Island, giving the Borough a civic
consciousness it seldom felt before." Although he stayed
out of public life, his impact was through his newspaper,
"its policies, the good causes it has espoused, the activities
it has supported, the harmful propositions it has opposed."

The Reverend Frederick Sutter, pastor of Trinity Lu-
theran Church for forty-three years, brought Wagner College to the Island and helped to pick its site on Grymes Hill.
Prime mover in the college's expansion, up to 1950, he had
been president of its board of trustees for thirty-two years.

Mr. and Mrs. William G. Willcox "as philanthropists, civic
workers, educators and pioneers in the field of better race
relations gave unstintingly of their time, energies, talents and
money for Staten Island."

Although not on the *Advance's* "First Ten," other individuals were named in 1950. The Right Reverend Charles A.
Cassidy, once "dean" of the Island's Catholic clergy and pastor
of St. Peter's Church. George L. Egbert, a Tompkinsville mer-

chant, a founder of the Chamber of Commerce, and chairman of Local School Board 53, on which he'd then served for fifty-two years. William W. Wirt Mills, civil leader and, as City Commissioner of the old Department of Plants and Structures, savior of the five-cent ferry fare.

Four members of the Pouch family—Alonzo B., Arnold C., Oscar G., and William H.—who contributed much through their American Dock Company and Pouch Terminals to the Island's commercial progress and civic betterment.

John Frederick Smith, "dean" of Island bankers and nationally known insurance executive, who gave freely of his time from a very busy life to act as financial adviser to "many poor persons."

Theodore H. Spratt, a vice president of the Corn Exchange Bank and Trust Company, had great influence on local industry and business and civic development. David J. Tysen, the Island's largest landowner, along with other activities, developed his vast properties, headed the Todt Hill iron mining area and gave Staten Island Hospital's Nurses' Home.

With the Island's constant population growth the question arises: can the *Advance* project a similar list when the borough reaches its seventy-fifth anniversary? Meanwhile, each year since 1962, when the paper named its first choice of "Women of Achievement," certain women as leaders in various fields of endeavor for community betterment have been cited at an enormous luncheon and presented with silver bowls, suitably engraved.

Among Islanders who achieved a different kind of fame was Richard Crowe who was brought up in Midland Beach and later acquired a handsome house along the beach at Eltingville. As manager of an Island branch of the National City Bank, he was a popular and active individual, frequently cited for his community services. Later he was promoted to the bank's branch at 195 Broadway, Manhattan. One afternoon, in the spring of 1949, Crowe walked into the bank vault and removed a total of $883,660 in a record theft. He carefully tucked his loot in a couple of large, leather traveling bags and started home. He crossed the ferry, chatting with friends on the way. Finding the bags too cumbersome to carry to his car in a nearby parking lot, he asked a traffic officer on duty at the Richmond Terrace crossing at Borough Hall to watch the bags till he could swing by and pick them up. The officer obliged, unaware of what he was guarding.

Later Crowe took most of his loot to Silver Mount Cemetery, where, for safety's sake, he buried it, carefully wrapped, in the family's lot before slipping away to Florida where he was eventually picked up. Because most of the money was returned, his prison term was short. He returned to the Island and after being, for a brief time, the subject of conversation he was forgotten.

Willie "the Actor" Sutton, who preferred violent methods in acquiring bank moneys, lived on the Island from 1947 to 1950. A meek and mild-appearing little man, he worked as a porter at Sea View Hospital, answering to the name of Eddie Lynch, while the FBI and police all over the country hunted for him. When he slipped out of Sea View following a particularly bold bank robbbery in Queens, fellow-workers couldn't believe that little Eddie was the notorious and dangerous bankrobber, Willie Sutton.

During World Wars I and II the Island, because of its strategic location in the harbor, was carefully watched by governmental agencies alerted for spies. There were frequent "spy scares" and reports of signals flashing from the hilltops to enemy submarines lurking outside the harbor. Bars on the East Shore at Tompkinsville and Stapleton frequented by ship crews and longshoremen were under constant FBI surveillance as were haunts of shipyard workers and longshoremen on the North Shore. It was in one of these in Port Richmond that a Nazi spy, Ernest Lehmitz, was caught. Living in Brighton Heights for several years he had worked in the bar-restaurant for months before the FBI's tireless agents, following the thinnest of clues, arrested him along with Erwin H. DeSpretter, another Nazi working on the Island. Both were convicted and given thirty-year sentences, but neither served his full time.

Although few were surprised, hundreds of Islanders were made uneasy in January, 1970, by published confirmation of the unpleasant fact that for years Cosa Nostra members had been living quietly in various residential areas. As of that date, twenty-seven were identified by name and address.

Along with the many individuals (already mentioned in previous chapters) who have lived and worked on the Island, were numerous poets, authors, musicians, critics and artists of national and international importance. If a complete list could be compiled it would certainly be a very very long one.

Those interested in the overall study of the Island's connection with the literary world and its various phases will be ever grateful and appreciative of Mabel Abbott's exhaustive research. Starting in 1932, Miss Abbott unearthed not only long lists of authors, poets, critics, dramatists and others who had some literary association with the Island but she discovered heretofore unknown bits such as that Edgar Allen Poe often visited his friend Richard Adams Locke here and seriously thought of using the Polly Bodine murder case as the basis of a mystery story. Richard Watson Gilder, poet, critic and editor, wrote some of the poems of his first book here in 1874. Maxim Gorky wrote "Mother" while staying at John Martin's Grymes Hill residence. Mrs. Cunliffe-Owen, a lady-in-waiting at the Austrian court as well as the author of best sellers, lived with her husband in the former LaBau mansion, now the Swedish Home. The Cunliffe-Owens also occupied the Ward house on Grymes Hill.

Edwin Arlington Robinson wrote parts of two plays while living in the Latourette house above Richmondtown. Theodore Dreiser, Julia Peterkin, Sam and Bella Spewack, Mildred Evans Gilman, Sholem Asch, Arthur Mason, E. L. Voynich and others were on Miss Abbott's list along with James Gould

Cozzens, Theodora DuBois, Lawton Mackall and Phyllis A. Whitney. With the Island so close to publishers and still a safe distance from distractions, it has been suggested that more writers are working quietly here and making more literary history than ever before.

In the world of painting Jasper Francis Cropsey, born at the family farm in Rossville in 1823, was the first native-born Staten Islander to achieve an international reputation in art. In recent years a sudden surge of interest in Cropsey and certain of his paintings caused prices to soar.

For more than a century, artists have been attracted to the Island because of its natural beauty, its simple living, and because of being within an hour of New York's art world. To list only a very few who lived and worked here would be William Page, Guy Pène duBois, Henry Schnakenberg, Percy Leason, Gilmer Petroff, William Hurd Lawrence, Robert Hallowell, Rockwell Kent, Ernest Roth, Ernest Beaumont, Albert Thompson Bricher, Ben Benn, Frederick W. Kost. . . .

World-famous architect Ernest Flagg had a magnificent estate in Dongan Hills, although the only local record of his work can be seen in his own residence, gatehouse, a few houses made from the serpentine rock quarried on his property and the Reformed Church in Huguenot. The Flagg mansion is now occupied by St. Charles Seminary.

Other nationally noted architects who found the Island a pleasant place to live were John Merven Carrère, designer of Borough Hall and the County Court House and a number of residences in New Brighton and St. George, still existing; Robert W. Gardner, who designed the Staten Island Museum and local residences; Henry Hobson Richardson, who lived in the house he designed and built in 1868 at the northeast corner of McLean and Lily Pond Avenues, Arrochar. It has been suggested that James Renwick was responsible for the remodeling of the Austen Cottage. Arthur Gilman designed St. John's Church—"the first church in America" at the Narrows

—Robert Upjohn did the Church of the Holy Comforter in Eltingville, now called St. Alban's Church. However, there's no record available to indicate that either Renwick or Upjohn lived on the Island. Nor, of course, did Frank Lloyd Wright although the Island does have a house of his design at 48 Manor Court on Lighthouse Hill.

Few Islanders are aware that Ruth St. Denis—"Miss Ruth" —when she lived here many years ago, was Ruthie Dennis. The Dennis house still stands south of Richmond Memorial Hospital in Princes Bay. The three Barrymores as children spent summers on the Island. In fact tradition has it that brother Lionel attended the Staten Island Academy when the family lived here.

Twentieth century international figures and Dongan Hills residents were Robert C. Stanley, Edward R. Stettinius and Edward R. Stettinius, Jr. Mr. Stanley, modestly listed in *Who's Who* as "mining engineer," was chairman of the board and president of International Nickel for many years and holder of innumerable honors and awards from foreign governments, learned societies and universities.

Prior to World War I, Mr. Stettinius headed giant corporations and his son's career after the family moved from the Island was distinguished—a General Motors executive, Chairman of the Board of United States Steel, Under Secretary of State under Cordell Hull, then Secretary of State, and, finally, U.S. representative to the United Nations.

Sir Edward Cunard's memory is kept alive as American representative of the famous steamship line because of his mansion, well publicized as a Wagner College building. In recent years the image of Cunard was kept particularly bright by William Y. Daly, general manager of Cunard in this country, whose community interests and activities had a great impact locally, particularly as first president of the Staten Island Mental Health Society. Another important shipping executive and administrator was Captain Granville Conway, an Island resident for forty years. Atlantic Coast director of the War

Shipping Administration following World War II, he was also appointed by President Truman as Director of Transportation for the National Security and Resources Board. At the time of his death in 1969 he was president of Cosmopolitan Shipping and Homes Lines and chairman of Commercial Tankers of Liberia.

Nor can Islanders ever forget two heroes who received the nation's highest award, the Congressional Medal of Honor: awarded posthumously to Pfc Joseph F. Merrell, Jr., of West Brighton, who was killed in Germany in 1945, and Navy Chaplain Vincent R. Capodanno of Elm Park, a Maryknoll priest, who, although wounded, gave his life in caring for marines dying on a battlefield in Vietnam. The eighteen-year-old soldier and the priest are both buried in St. Peter's Cemetery on Clove Road, West Brighton.

Looking Backward

Probably the first native Islander to achieve fame abroad was the Negro boy, Bill Richmond, a teenager in the household of the Reverend Richard Charlton, rector of the Church of St. Andrew in Richmondtown. Apparently Bill's flair for fighting—"milling" it was then called—attracted the attention of sports-minded British officers on the Island and particularly of Lord Hugh Percy, the lieutenant general who had covered the bloody retreat after the battle of Lexington. When Percy returned to England in 1777, the young fighter was taken along as his lordship's servant.

Boxiana, published in London in 1812, provides considerable information on "this man of colour," along with his portrait. He was sent to school in Yorkshire and later apprenticed to a York cabinetmaker and rose to journeyman. His first fight in England was with George Moore of the 19th Regiment. His first fight in London was in the fields near White Conduit House, where he showed his skill as a "scientific fighter." Noted for his clean appearance, Bill was still fighting when he was fifty years old, although it was said he looked no more than thirty-five and had kept his weight of 10 stone 12 pounds.

Along with his reputation as a fighter, he was noted as the prosperous owner of a popular inn, "The Horse and Dolphin." He was famous as a trainer and it was said he'd instructed hundreds in the fine art of boxing. He was also a good cricketer. To quote *Boxiana*—"Richmond is entitled to a respectable niche among the portraits of first rate heroes of the milling art."

While there is no evidence, recent writers have suggested that Elizabeth Bayley Seton, the first native-born American beatified by the Roman Catholic Church, was born on Staten Island, possibly in the rectory of the Church of St. Andrew, her mother's family home. That she lived on the Island as a child and young woman is well known. Her grandfather was the Reverend Richard Charlton, D.D., of St. Andrew's. Her father was Dr. Richard Bayley, first health officer of the Port of New York. Her fifth child, Catherine, was born in Dr. Bayley's house at Quarantine. Her journal indicates that she loved the Island and had many friends here.

When Dr. Bayley died of yellow fever in August, 1801, it was Mrs. Seton who circumvented the ban (because of the plague) of moving his body over Island roads to St. Andrew's churchyard by having the coffin taken by boat through the Kills and creeks to within a short distance from the church. At that time she wrote of her desire to be buried in that "sacred resting place." But her destiny decreed otherwise.

Following her husband's tragic death in Italy, where he had gone in search of health, she became a convert to Catholicism in 1805. Ultimately she formed the Sisters of Charity, the first congregation of nuns in this country. Mother Seton never returned to the Island, but many years later eight Island schools and St. Vincent's Hospital were staffed by nuns of the order which she had founded in Baltimore.

The vestry of the Episcopal Church of St. Andrew granted permission to the Sisters of Charity to place a bronze plaque on the outer wall of the edifice near the entrance. This was

done early in 1963. It reads: "IN MEMORY OF THE RELA-
TIVES OF ELIZABETH BAYLEY SETON WHO ARE
BURIED IN THE CHURCHYARD." Listed are her grand-
parents, Reverend Richard Charlton, D.D. and Mary Bayeux
Charlton; her parents, Dr. Richard Bayley and Catherine
Charlton Bayley; her sister, Mary Bayley Post and her
brother-in-law, Dr. Wright Post.

The plaque also records that it was erected by the Sisters
of Charity . . . "in honor of their founder Venerable Mother
Elizabeth Bayley Seton."

The Island was a happy place of retirement for army and
navy officers. They added zest to local society. Rear Admiral
John Drake Sloat, who had achieved fame by boldly taking
Monterey prior to hostilities in the Mexican War and later
took possession of San Francisco for the United States, lived
in a Gothic cottage on Richmond Terrace between Franklin
and York Avenues. Brigadier General Ranald Slidell Mackenzie, noted Indian fighter and hero of a television series
sixty years after his death, lived with his sister, Mrs. Matthew
Galbraith Perry, in a house at Henderson and Lafayette Avenues, now the site of Public School 40, New Brighton.

The Benhams, Commander Timothy Green Benham and
his son Rear Admiral Andrew Ellicot Kennedy Benham, rate
special mention. The Commander was a hero in the naval
attack on Vera Cruz in 1847 and his son of higher rank had a
distinguished naval career. The U.S. Navy named two destroy-
ers for the Admiral. The first *Benham*, launched in 1913, was
a torpedo-boat destroyer. The second *U.S.S. Benham*, also a
destroyer, was launched in 1938 and saw considerable action in
World War II. The Admiral's daughter, Edith Benham Helm,
a popular figure in Washington, had the distinction of serving
as social secretary to three First Ladies—the second Mrs.
Woodrow Wilson, Mrs. Franklin D. Roosevelt and Mrs.
Harry S. Truman. The glimpses of Staten Island given in
Mrs. Helm's *The Captains and the Kings*, particularly of the
Benhams' huge stone house on the Arthur Kill Road midway

between Richmond and Green Ridge, have special charm. Among the treasures there was Audubon's *The Birds of America.* "As a child I was told," Mrs. Helm wrote, "that Audubon was a friend of my grandfather's and that he tramped all over Staten Island in his study of birds. And when I was shown the picture of the marsh wren, it was with the information that it had been painted right there on Staten Island near the old house."

Island historians record that Jenny Lind "made her home on Staten Island whenever circumstances would permit, and became quite intimate with many of our people. She was very fond of riding over the Island. Todt Hill being one of her favorite routes." It is also happily recorded that she gave several concerts in the Pavilion Hotel. A noted twentieth century successor to the "Swedish Nightingale" is Eileen Farrell, who lived for several years with her husband and children in a handsome house on Grymes Hill.

Max Maretzek, the impresario who introduced Italian opera in New York's Academy of Music in 1854, had a comfortable house in the South Shore overlooking Pleasant Plains. He lived there till his death in 1898. His grave is in Moravian Cemetery. Thirty years later, world-famous harpist Maude Morgan also lived in Pleasant Plains. In her charming brick house, converted from a small ice house on a private estate, beside a pond, she gave many annual Twelfth Night parties that are still happy memories for those fortunate enough to have been there.

Of the clergy ministering for more than two centuries to Island congregations, some went on to higher office. Two rectors of St. Andrew's—Dr. Richard Channing Moore and Dr. Charles Sumner Birch—became bishops of the Protestant Episcopal Church. The Reverend Francis Asbury, the first American Methodist bishop, made Staten Island his first "circuit." Bishop John F. Hurst and Bishop Henry Spellmeyer were formerly ministers of Trinity Methodist Church. Bishop Spellmeyer had also been minister of Kingsley Methodist.

Moravian Bishop Alan W. Schattschneider had served previously at New Dorp Moravian Church and Bishop Carl J. Helmich had been pastor of Castleton Hill Moravian. A Prince of the Roman Catholic Church, John Cardinal Farley was once a priest of St. Peter's Church, New Brighton; so, too, was Archbishop James Roosevelt Bayley of Baltimore, a convert to Catholicism and a cousin of Mother Seton. And the Reverend Robert I. Gannon, S.J., president of Fordham University for thirteen years still has close ties to Staten Island.

Islanders take pride too in the Stapleton Union American Methodist Church on Tompkins Avenue. With its origin traced back to the end of the Revolutionary War it is considered one of the oldest independent Negro churches in the world.

The Island was a haven for such political exiles as Jeremiah O'Donovan-Rossa, one of the leaders of Irish revolutionists; General Joseph Karge, a Polish patriot who had escaped a Russian death sentence, served as an officer in the Union Army and later lived in Livingston. Another Civil War officer on the Island was Gustav von Struve, an escapee from 1848 German revolutionary movements. But, without doubt, the most famous political exile who sought security on the Island was Antonio López de Santa Anna, former "Emperor" of Mexico and in most American minds "the Butcher of the Alamo."

Through the assistance of Gilbert L. Thompson, a son-in-law of Vice President Tompkins, Santa Anna escaped from Vera Cruz on Thompson's three-masted schooner anchored in the harbor. Eventually he arrived safely on the Island with the Thompsons and lived for a while in a mansard-roofed house on Manor Road, at the northwest corner of the present Forest Avenue. Probably no other Island visitor ever used Santa Anna's way of departure, which involved his being smuggled away nailed up in a piano crate to avoid capture by Mexican agents. Sheriff Abram Winant cantered beside the wagon as it rumbled down to the waterfront with the crate. Soon its was safely aboard the waiting schooner for the long voyage back to Mexico. But despite all these precautions Santa Anna was captured at sea and never did get back his former power.

Nor can the fact be forgotten that Staten Island was home to four individuals of utmost importance in the early days of photography: Dr. John W. Draper, Matthew B. Brady, Timothy O'Sullivan and E. Alice Austen. Howard Henderson Cleaves of Eltingville, renowned wild life photographer, should be a present-day inclusion to this august group.

Dr. Draper, professor of chemistry and physiology at New York University, is said to have discovered while living on Staten Island certain photographic methods superior to Daguerre's for portrait work and took the first satisfactory picture of a human face. The year was 1840.

Matthew B. Brady, famous Civil War photographer, lived on Grymes Hill. Timothy O'Sullivan, a Brady assistant during the war and later a noted photographer in his own right for a great series of pictures of the West and of Panama, was the subject of a long due biography in 1966. He died on the Island and was buried in St. Peter's Cemetery.

For well over sixty years, life had been extremely kind to Alice Austen. But this was before the stock market crash of 1929 engulfed her in a downward spiral that finally ended by her becoming a pauper in the city's poorhouse, politely known as the Farm Colony. There, at the age of eighty-three, ill and crippled with arthritis, she waited stoically for death.

When her possessions were being sold, the Staten Island Historical Society purchased thousands of glass negatives, 8 by 10 inches, that Miss Austen had taken since she first started with a cumbersome camera in the early 1880s. In the late 1940s all the Historical Society's activities were carried on by volunteers so it was a long, long time before Miss Austen's negatives and prints were finally in order. Well aware of the greatness of the collection, the Historical Society attempted to raise some money by selling rights to certain negatives. Finally, through the efforts of Oliver Jensen—who had learned of the collection while hunting for material for a book of his own—*Life* and *Holiday* and other publications paid for rights to publish some of the photographs. And Miss Austen was able to leave the Farm Colony and spend her last days in a nursing home in Livingston, formerly one of the Island's elegant residences and where she had attended many elaborate parties as a young lady.

Honors poured in on Alice Austen following *Life's* first eight-page spread in its September 24, 1951 issue. She was interviewed on radio and television and feature stories ran in newspapers throughout the country. "Alice Austen Day" —October 7, 1951—was observed by a large reception for hundreds of Miss Austen's old friends and the opening of an exhibition in the Historical Museum, Richmondtown, of a few of Miss Austen's photographs.

Along with her glass negatives and thousands of prints, Miss Austen's cameras are on display in the museum. A group composed of Islanders and New Yorkers—Friends of the Alice Austen House—in recent years have been seeking to raise funds to save the old house and grounds along the Narrows: the house to be used as a photographic museum honoring Alice Austen; the grounds, along with the adjoining property of four acres, formerly used by the New York Yacht Club, to become a park, with a waterfront promenade from Hylan Boulevard to Fort Wadsworth.

The family of President John Tyler, found pleasant living in the handsome mansion at the junction of Broadway and Clove Road. The present address is Tyler Avenue and the former spacious lawns are now occupied by little houses. The Tylers' neighbors, the Barretts, lived a short distance down Broadway on the opposite side of the street. Present occupants of that site are the animals, fish, birds and reptiles of the Staten Island Zoo in Barrett Park, now among the country's finest zoos.

There are still Islanders who remember watching polo played on the Manor Farm field, later used by Troop F of the National Guard cavalry preparing for its service on the Mexican border prior to World War I. The turreted brick "armory" was erected on part of the site following World War I. The massive structure is now headquarters for Troops A-B-C, First Squadron, 101st Cavalry. There are other Islanders who talk about DeJonge's paper factory when it was on the old Richmond Turnpike between Louis Street and Austin Place, and the fireworks factories in the fields along "the Boulevard" between Midland Avenue and Old Town Road and another on Richmond Avenue at Graniteville, not far from Ettlinger's box factory, where all kinds of boxes, especially jewelry boxes, were made. And there was also Jewett's white lead factory along the shore in Port Richmond; and S.S. White at Princes Bay, busy making a variety of "things" for the dental profession. Nor should one of the world's first airplane factories set up by Charles R. Witteman around 1907 in the Little Clove on Ocean Terrace be forgotten. By 1915, records indicate that his company had turned out five hundred biplane gliders. "Red Devils" were also built there for Captain Thomas Baldwin, an Islander who gave flying exhibitions throughout the country. Mr. Witteman and a brother also had a flying field on the Island, set up in 1912 at Oakwood Heights. In need of greater space in 1917 the factory was moved to Teterboro, N.J. Giuseppe Bellanca, noted aviator and airplane designer, was building planes in the 1920s in one of the old World War I shipping building areas at Mariners Harbor. He lived on Sunset Hill off West Brighton's Bard Avenue during this period.

So that Islanders would be reminded of Aaron Burr, Vice President of the United States 1801–1805, the Staten Island Chapter, Daughters of the American Revolution, placed a tablet on the building in Port Richmond, then an inn, where he died on September 14, 1836. Burr, who had tied with Jefferson for the Presidency in 1801, was a popular figure to many Islanders, who took special pleasure in visiting him during his last few days in Winant's Inn, overlooking the Kill van Kull. Displayed in the Historical Museum, Richmondtown, is a combined chair-and-table desk said to have been designed by Burr.

Members of the Staten Island Philatelist Society delight in the knowledge that theirs is the oldest stamp club in the country.

Staten Island's Claim To Fame by Vernon B. Hampton, published in 1925 and long out of print, notes that Jacob Dolson Cox once lived in Port Richmond as a teenager. Later he became a major general in the Union Army, Governor of Ohio, and Secretary of the Interior under President Grant. John C. Fremont, the Pathfinder, who had been governor of California and the newly formed Republican Party's presidential candidate in 1856, lived on the Island several times during his career, the last residence being in New Brighton.

Two other governors who had ties with the Island were Caleb Lyons who had been the governor of Idaho Territory and William Ludlow, an army officer who became Military and Civil Governor of Havana, Cuba, in 1898. Perhaps it's stretching things a bit to list General Ludlow, since he lived on the Island only during his tour of duty in charge of fortifications and river and harbor work of army engineers. During those years he lived in Tompkinsville. But Caleb Lyon, by buying the Ross Castle in Rossville and renaming it Lyon's Castle, living there and entertaining with considerable splendor for a number of years, made quite an impact on local society.

The Jewish community on the Island was recently described as "a small and old one." It's difficult to pinpoint the exact date when the first Jewish family came to make a home on the Island. But, by 1852 the Greenwald family was living in Port Richmond where Moses Greenwald, head of the family, continued as a successful and important merchant on the North Shore for forty-five years. Later his son, Abram Greenwald, had an important part in local public and cultural affairs, especially as "the father of the Jewish Community Center." Third, fourth and fifth generations of Island Jewish families today continue active in business and professions and all phases of community life. The Congregation B'nai Jeshurun, incorporated in 1888, is considered the oldest of the Island's ten Jewish religious organizations.

In the world of sports the Island had such stars as Elmer Ripley in basketball; Bobby Thomson and Matty McIntyre in World Series baseball; and Abel Kiviat, who ran with the 1912 Olympic team. Percy Duncan Haughton, the great "P.D."—a star in all sports and inventor of the "Harvard System"—was born in New Brighton in 1876 and spent his early life on the Island. Another native-born Islander who brought immense influence in collegiate athletics was Charles W. Kennedy whose ties with the Island remained close during the eighty-seven years of his life.

Dr. Kennedy's book, *Collegiate Athletics*, held educators responsible for the proper development and direction of their athletic programs as with any other part of college life. Head of Princeton University's English department for many years and Murray Professor of English literature emeritus at the time of his death in 1969, and chairman of Princeton's faculty committee on athletics for nine years—a post designated today as athletic director—Dr. Kennedy's career was a prime example of what his *Collegiate Athletics* stressed.

The achievements of Anning S. Prall of Westerleigh gave Staten Island another claim to a "first" when he was appointed the first chairman of the new Federal Communications Committee. He had been elected to Congress in 1923. Prior to that he had served three terms—1919, 1920 and 1921—as president of New York City's Board of Education.

In June, 1969, the *Advance* reported that the Island had only three survivors of the Spanish American War: William Gaylor, Harry Hansen and Henry Poulsen. But the Island also had another resident who was a veteran of that war, ninety-five-year-old Samuel A. Browne, and a few weeks later the

Advance published a feature story about this soldier, a Negro, who had served his country for three years, part of this service in the Philippines. Unfortunately, when he had tried many years ago to join local veteran groups he had been rejected because of his color. In 1924, Mr. Browne and his wife, a teacher in Public School 12, Concord, had met with bitter opposition when they had bought a house on Fairview Avenue near Castleton Corners. For months a city policeman guarded the Brownes and their four children from attack. Bitter and cruel actions had been endured over those first years, but the danger finally passed and eventually the Brownes were accepted by the neighbors. More recently, Samuel A. Browne, III, a grandson, won a Purple Heart with the Marines in Vietnam. There will be no rejection if and when *he* wishes to join a veterans' organization on his return.

Landmarks and Restorations

Among the thousands of newcomers to Staten Island—post office figures indicate a thousand a month—fleeing the noise and congestion of older sections of the city, many look to the past for their homes: well-built houses with the turrets and towers of the Victorian era, and with large rooms, high ceilings and fireplaces; others with mansard roofs and verandas and plenty of room outside for gardening and children at play. Young professionals have been attracted to New Brighton and Stapleton, both integrated for years, where there's a definite "restoration renaissance."

The Staten Island Historical Society's Richmondtown Restoration has sparked a tremendous interest in the past. And, in recent years, the city's Landmarks Preservation Commission has proposed or designated nearly a hundred structures throughout the Island as "landmarks." A court battle rages with the trustees of Sailors' Snug Harbor and the Commission over the preservation of what the latter designates as "a great and enduring architectural masterpiece . . . one of the most notable Greek revival compositions in the United States."

The trustees, however, are quoted as considering the old buildings—now the homes of more than two hundred old sailors—as "wasteful, unimaginative, inefficient, antiquated firetraps which should be torn down to make way for the future." They prefer to tear down four of the buildings and put up three, modern ten-story apartment buildings for the "aged, decrepit and wornout sailors" who are spending their remaining years at Snug Harbor because of the terms of the will of Captain Robert Richard Randall who died in 1801. The will drawn by Alexander Hamilton and Daniel D. Tompkins, left a 21-acre farm in Manhattan along Broadway at Tenth Street and extending from the Bowery to Fifth Avenue, for the establishment of a "Home for Aged Decrepit and Wornout Sailors." With the tremendous increase in Manhattan's land values, the "Home" was set up on Staten Island along the Kills on 140 acres of land, salt meadow and marsh. The first inmates arrived in August, 1833. The income from Manhattan rentals made Sailors' Snug Harbor one of the wealthiest institutions in the country.

Thirteen more landmarks—all in Richmondtown—were designated by the Commission in September, 1969. Prior to that, the *Voorlezer's* House had received due recognition for being the oldest elementary schoolhouse extant in the United States by the presentation of a plaque from H.R.H Crown Princess Juliana, the present Queen of the Netherlands; furthermore, by the National Park Service official designation as a national historic landmark.

The Richmondtown Restoration has been described as "a living museum spanning more than two centuries of American history and readily accessible to twenty million people . . . the first 'Peoples' Restoration' in the nation, since the urban underprivileged as well as the affluent will be able to visit Richmondtown Restoration easily by subway, ferryboat and bus."

The Restoration started in a very modest way in 1939 when gifts from certain Staten Island Historical Society members "saved" the ancient house by enabling the Society to acquire and restore it. The old structure had been erected prior to 1696 for "the *Voorlezer*" who served as lay reader and teacher for the few Dutch families living in that center area of the Island.

Over the years the dream of a Restoration grew when other original buildings in the former county seat were acquired with the surrounding land. Prime mover in the project was Loring McMillen, an engineer in the New York Telephone Company, whose great hobby was old houses and local history. He also held the unpaid office of borough historian. Aided and encouraged by other local historians and Island leaders, such as William T. Davis, Charles W. Leng, Cornelius G. Kolff, Mrs. T. Livingstone Kennedy, the Reverend Lefferd M. A. Haughwout, Tom Garrett, and Vernon B. Hampton, and by a volunteer group of his colleagues in the telephone company, the project grew. The Historical Society turned over its acreage to the City of New York in the early 1950s and the Restoration is now a joint endeavor of the Park Department and the Historical Society.

Twenty buildings of the thirty-six to be placed in the Restoration are already on their sites. With a recent grant from the Triborough Bridge and Tunnel Authority of a quarter of a million dollars a saw mill and mill pond have been placed on original sites, and roads and a greatly needed parking area were installed in 1969. Eleven houses of historic interest and architectural importance are being moved in to save them from the onslaught of real estate development. Among these is a house erected by Vice President Tompkins as a wedding present for one of his children. This is a beautiful example of the Federal period. Another handsome house scheduled to be moved soon is Greek Revival, a two-storied and porticoed house formerly used as the physician's residence in Sailors' Snug Harbor.

The Britton Cottage, once the home of Nathaniel Lord Britton, noted geologist, botanist and director-in-chief for many years of the New York Botanical Garden, is now being restored after a 4-mile moving over Island roads from New

Dorp Beach, where it had stood since 1677. Close by stands the Lake-Tysen farmhouse erected in 1740. Moving it through Island streets for three miles took three days of careful manoeuvring.

Among the buildings "already there" are the "Treasure House," erected in 1700 (Major André is said to have written his will in the house before setting out to meet Benedict Arnold); the Third Court House, dated 1838; the County Clerk's and Surrogate's office used from 1848 to 1920, now the Historical Museum. Also completed are the Stephens House and General Store, the Bennett House and a carriage house in which part of the Society's fine carriage collection is displayed under the direction of Paul H. Downing, an Island resident for many years. Mr. Downing is noted as the carriage consultant at Williamsburg, consultant of the National Park Service, editor of *Carriage* and the only American member of the Worshipful Company of Coach Makers and Coach Harness Makers of London, chartered by Charles II.

Other individuals of national prominence associated with the Richmondtown Restoration as officers or trustees are Robert Moses, Honorary Chairman; Amy Vanderbilt, Chairman; Richard T. (Dick) Button, President; Mrs. Norman H. Donald, Mrs. John Kean, Mrs. Robert C. Stanley, Mrs. Charles Deere Wiman, Richard N. Colhoun, Clarence Francis, Albert Hart, Stewart Huston, Edward L. Love and Chauncey D. Stillman.

The Historical Society's traditional "Old Home Day" held each year in October brings thousands of visitors—twenty thousand were said to have flocked in for the 1969 "Old Home Day." They watched demonstrations of blacksmithing, spinning, weaving, candle making, cider making and fireplace cooking. There was also the excitement of watching a break, drawn by a pair of handsome bay horses, moving along the village streets and later the rattle of guns fired in a sham battle of Civil War buffs. The sudden wail of the siren atop the volunteer firemen's station closeby on Richmond Road added further to the excitement. This group, Richmond Engine Company, No. 1, and the Ocean Hook and Ladder Company, No. 1, at Travis, are the last two volunteer fire companies left in the city.

Since New York Mayor John V. Lindsay recently announced that the Richmond Restoration would be the city's official salute to the Bicentennial Anniversary of the United States in 1976, the Staten Island Historical Society and the Richmondtown Restoration (the latter being the fund-raising arm for the project) are accelerating their efforts to complete the Restoration by that year.

Meanwhile, hundreds visit Richmondtown every week. Some for the first time. Others to watch the progress. Thousands of school children from every borough and from schools in New Jersey, Connecticut and Long Island came during the year to see how Americans lived nearly three hundred years ago.

Transit Hub and Village Greens

A 66-page "Master Plan" for Staten Island, prepared by the City Planning Commission was "unveiled" on the first of March, 1970. It was the first of five to be issued for each borough of the city. It wasn't done in the traditional style of mapping street networks, specific communities and commercial and industrial areas. Instead it stressed "coherent development," emphasizing the relationship between transportation and development. Charts, graphs, maps and photographs, along with about 25,000 words, expressed concrete recommendations and predicted the Island's future, especially in "land use composite evaluation and future land use plans." Some Islanders believed the Master Plan stressed quantity, not quality.

Donald H. Elliott, City Planning Commission Chairman, explained that the plan was an attempt to "comprehend" the city and the Island . . . "This is the first time all this information has been put in one place . . . It recognizes that we must work with the topography and acknowledges the SIRT as a transportation spine. It considers the relationships between open space, transportation and housing . . ."

A previous traffic study done by the Port of New York

Smith, D.

Staten Island; gateway to
New York

4/18 Mrs. Leiter

Authority admits that Staten Island has become the hub of transportation movement in New York City. Bridges, highways, expressways and the "Container Revolution" were credited with giving new life to the waterfront, particularly to East Shore piers at Stapleton and a vast new containership terminal on the Arthur Kill.

A bright era for Staten Island and its commuters was predicted on December 18, 1969, with the City's acquiring from the Chesapeake & Ohio-Baltimore & Ohio Railroad its Staten Island Rapid Transit for the sum of $3,500,001. This added another commuter line to be administered by the Metropolitan Transportation Authority. The railroad will continue using Island tracks for freight service. Fifty-two new air-conditioned cars are scheduled to replace the forty-seven battered veterans used since 1925 when SIRT became electrified. The cars will ply the 14.3-mile track from St. George to Tottenville through the South Shore. And when the track bed is renovated a top speed of 80 miles an hour is predicted.

Baltimore & Ohio tracks along the North Shore were in constant use during World Wars I and II in moving thousands of troops to Island piers for transport overseas. Millions of tons of arms, tanks and munitions crossed over the Arthur Kill Railroad Bridge to waiting freighters at Stapleton. At dawn one morning Prime Minister Winston Churchill came ashore and quietly departed via a waiting Baltimore & Ohio train. Few Islanders were aware that the great man had slipped through on his way to a secret conference with President Roosevelt in Washington. Because of this visit the Island was facetiously called "the backdoor to America." But there was no secrecy years later when Queen Elizabeth II, also using the Baltimore & Ohio, arrived with Prince Philip. Crowds lined Bay Street while the royal motorcade drove slowly along to a special ferry that took them across the Bay. Was the Queen aware that her great-grandfather Edward VII, when Prince of Wales, traveling incognito as Baron Renfrew,

danced till dawn at an elaborate ball given in his honor at
Ross Castle in Rossville, during his American tour in 1860?

Members of the Dutch royal family have visited friends on
the Island over the years and the Crown Princess Beatrix
was welcomed in an enormous reception at Borough Hall
and made an "Honorary Citizen of Staten Island" during the
Hudson-Champlain Celebration. The Reverend Dr. Winfield
Burggraaff, an Island Reformed Church minister, is also a
special tie of the royal family to the Island since, as a chaplain
for the Dutch Navy in World War II, he christened the little
daughter of the then Crown Princess Juliana, when the baby
was born in Canada.

In spite of the great bridge across the Narrows, ferry service
to Manhattan remains essential. At a five-cent fare, twenty-
three million passengers were carried in 1969. Studies are
frequently made. Should there be a rapid transit tunnel under
the Bay to Manhattan? A tunnel and surface rapid transit
route via Bayonne? A transit route over the Verrazano-Narrows Bridge? None of the studies has dragged out the plan
for a subway tunnel from St. George to Brooklyn. A plan
that started in the early 1920s and progressed to a shaft being
sunk at St. George, with rights-of-way mapped and taken
through the Island. This shaft remained for a quarter of a
century till the ferry terminal was rebuilt following the holocaust of June 25, 1946.

At the end of 1970 the water troubles of Islanders living in
the South Shore area will be over, or so city officials say.
The Richmond Water Tunnel, costing $40,514,509, will be
opened by that time and will deliver two to three million
gallons of water daily: the source being the great Catskill
and Adirondack watershed used by the city. The tremendous
underground storage tanks installed at Silver Lake have caused
much anguish and annoyance to residents of the area.

Miller Field at New Dorp Beach was named for the first
aviator with an American unit killed in France during World
War I. Acquired by the Army in 1919, and used over half

a century as an air coast defense station, a testing place for Admiral Byrd's plane used in Antarctica, for Civil Air Patrol and Green Beret units, National Guard aviation and tank company units and other purposes, Miller Field is now the target for all kinds of proposals. The midair collision over the field on December 16, 1960, between a United Airlines DC 8 and a TWA Super Constellation, which took 134 lives, will always be remembered as one of the greatest of air disasters.

What has been described as "the most ambitious privately financed housing development in Staten Island history" was announced on March 4, 1970. "Arden Heights" on a 160-acre tract in Huguenot, adjacent to the South Shore Golf Course, will comprise nine "villages" with two thousand dwelling units. The project is owned by Loew's Corporation of the hotel-theater chain. The cost involves a 100-million-dollar investment. Called "Village Greens," town houses in clusters ranging from seven to a dozen will be grouped around garden areas. There will be thirteen dwelling units to an acre, but no through traffic, no conventional street grid. According to the plan, the rolling woodland of the site will be "preserved in its natural charm."

The Bridge

The Island's backbone of serpentine rock stretches from St. George to Richmondtown in a range of hills called Fort, Pavilion, Ward, Grymes, Emerson, Todt, Dongan, Lighthouse and, finally, Richmond.

Fort Hill was so named because of British fortifications set up there during the Revolution; Pavilion Hill because of the popular Pavilion at its top; Ward for the family of that name who lived there; and Grymes for the family whose residence "Capo di Monte" literally crowned the hilltop.

Emerson Hill honored Judge William Emerson, whose more famous brother, Ralph Waldo Emerson, was said to have been a frequent visitor to the Judge's "Snuggery", described as a low, brown house on Richmond Road, Concord. In 1843 Henry David Thoreau lived with the Emersons as a tutor, and his comments on the Island are still remembered and quoted.

Todt Hill, all of 409.2 feet in altitude, is proudly labeled the highest point on the coast from Maine to Florida. Dongan Hills, named for the Colonial Governor Thomas Dongan, is considered the Island's finest residential section. Lighthouse Hill obviously received its name from the Staten Island light-

house, a major aid to ships navigating the Ambrose Channel
and a welcome sight to all ships entering New York Harbor.
Also on Lighthouse Hill is the Jacques Marchais Center of
Tibetan Art which displays the largest Tibetan collections
in the world outside of Tibet. Further west lies Richmond
Hill, part of Latourette Park and Golf Course, overlooking
the Church of St. Andrew and Richmondtown.

Staten Island's four bridges—Goethals, Outerbridge, Bayonne and the Verrazano-Narrows—have been described as
"an Othmar Ammann lover's paradise." They were all constructed under his design supervision. The Goethals Bridge
from Holland Hook to Elizabeth, New Jersey, was named
for General George W. Goethals, builder of the Panama
Canal, the Port of Authority's first chairman and its con-
sulting engineer when he died in 1928. That same year the
bridge was opened as was the Outerbridge Crossing between
Tottenville and Perth Amboy. This structure was named for
Eugene H. Outerbridge, a former Island resident and Port of
Authority chairman from 1921 to 1924. The Bayonne Bridge,
going over the Kills from Port Richmond to Bayonne, was
the longest steel-arch bridge in the world when it was opened
to traffic on November 15, 1931.

Eighty-one years after a link across the water between
Staten Island and Brooklyn was first proposed the great
Verrazano-Narrows Bridge was opened for traffic on November 21, 1964. The 4,260-foot length of its main span made it
the world's longest span. The length of the suspended structure is 6,690 feet and, including approaches, the total length
is 13,700 feet. That same year Harper & Row published Gay
Talese's exciting and fascinating story of its building. The
lives of thousands of people were affected by the bridge.
Families on both sides of the water were forced to move and
find new homes. Tradesmen had to relocate or go out of business. Before the bridge builders took over wreckers and bulldozers swept away hundreds of buildings in mountains of dust
and debris. The bridge builders themselves were a fabulous

lot, particularly the Indians and Newfoundlanders. Especially beautiful drawings of all phases of the construction, done on the site by Lili Rethi, F.R.S.A., add further to the book's value, as do the photographs of Bruce Davidson.

The bridge completed the arrangement of the so-called southern by-pass for the arterial highway system girding Manhattan and a new pattern for the metropolitan area emerged. Pressure and traffic jams on Hudson River crossings have lessened considerably as the bridge provides a vital link in the northeast megalopolis.

As a revenue producer, the Verrazano-Narrows Bridge has led in the Triborough Bridge and Tunnel Authority's eight bridge and tunnel complexes. Because of the tremendous traffic increase, the second level of the bridge was opened on June 28, 1969, eleven years ahead of schedule; thus increasing the capacity of the bridge's twelve traffic lanes to carry forty-eight million cars a year. More than one hundred million cars crossed in the first five years of operation. On Easter Sunday, 1969, one hundred thousand cars passed through the toll booths. Often lines of cars stretched for five miles along Brooklyn's Belt Parkway and the Staten Island Expressway that day, waiting to cross over.

That the bridge has changed life on Staten Island none can dispute. To outsiders the Island always had a way of life a step or two removed from the rest of the city because of its isolation. There are those who say that the Island, as the city's last frontier, a city within a city, has a fresh and splendid potential for development as a residential and recreational area.

Whether planners and developers will use this potential wisely and well or squander it recklessly, motivated by greed, will be determined within the next decade. By then—by 1980 —the "new" Staten Island is expected to emerge. The "old" Staten Island, having lost its flavor and character, will be no more.

Old Place Names

ANDROVETTEVILLE An 1856 name for the area later known as Kreischerville and Charleston.

ANNADALE This Staten Island Railroad station received this name circa 1860, honoring Mrs. Anna S. Seguine.

ARENTSVILLE For a brief period Tottenville bore this name.

ARLINGTON A Staten Island Rapid Transit Railroad station near Mariners' Harbor.

ARROCHAR Originally named about 1880 as the estate of W. W. MacFarland, near Fort Wadsworth.

BAY CITY Dr. Elliott's projected "city" along the water front in 1857.

BAY VIEW A post office on the East Shore at Clifton from 1858 to 1863.

BENTLEY An early name for Tottenville.

BLAZING STAR An early name for the Rossville area.

BLOOMFIELD Once a cluster of houses known as Watchogue.

BLOOMINGVIEW An 1846 name for Huguenot.

BRIGHTON HEIGHTS Originally the area along the present St. Marks Place, St. George.

BRISTOL Occasionally for a brief period in the 1840s this name appeared on maps designating the present Port Richmond.

BULL'S HEAD Acquired its name from a tavern with a sign carrying a bull's head. A popular Tory meeting place during the Revolution.

BURIAL PLACE The earliest name for the present Port Richmond.

BUTCHERVILLE A few houses on the Watchogue Road near the Willowbrook Road.

CASTLETON CORNERS The crossing of Manor Road and the old Richmond Turnpike, now Victory Boulevard.

CEDAR GROVE Close to the foot of New Dorp Lane and later the site of the Cedar Grove Beach Club.

CENTERVILLE An 1850 map designation for Castleton Corners.

CHARLESTON Received its name in World War I because of feeling against the German "Kreischerville."

CHELSEA A little settlement along the Arthur Kill on the west part of the Island. Once called "Peanutville" and, during the Revolution, Pralltown.

CITYVILLE In the 1830's a post office name for Factoryville.

CLIFTON This little East Shore settlement was developed in 1837. Nearby was Vanderbilt's Landing.

CLOVE The Clove came from the Dutch "Het Kloven," the cleft formed by Emerson and Grymes Hills at Concord. The land so designated stretched into the wide valley northward.

CONCORD Said to have been named by Emerson and Thoreau about 1845. Previously the section was Dutch Farms.

COURT HOUSE An early name for the railroad station which became Oakwood Heights. An even earlier name was Club House.

CUCKOLDSTOWN A pre-Revolution name for the county seat at Richmond, said to have evolved from cockleshells.

DECKER TOWN Travis once had this name because so many Deckers lived there.

DECKER'S FERRY Important during the Revolution. Later Port Richmond.

DONGAN HILLS Became a popular designation for a large area which formerly included Garretson's, a portion of Old Town and the hills going up from Richmond Road.

DOVER The Island's first permanent settlement became Dover following the English conquest of New Netherland. A second Dover has been placed near the present Egbertville.

EDGEWATER Incorporated in 1866 as an East Shore village.

EELTOWN A part of Pleasant Plains had this name in the middle of the 1800s.

EGBERTVILLE Old maps show that this area at Richmond Road and Rockland Avenue was also called Morgan's Corners, Young Ireland, New Dublin and Tipperary Corners.

ELLIOTTVILLE Dr. Samuel MacKenzie Elliott's territory. Later Livingston.

ELM PARK   Named for the elm trees that surrounded Dr. John
T. Harrison's house on the Shore Road, west of Port Rich-
mond. Called Jacksonville in 1829 and Lowville 20 years later.
A ferry landing and railroad station.

ELTINGVILLE   This area had two names before being named for
the Elting family. South Side was the post office up to 1872;
then Sea Side a year later.

EMERSON HILL   When Judge William Emerson, brother of the
famous Ralph Waldo Emerson, arrived to live here in 1843 the
hill was soon named for him.

ERASTINA   As a humorous gesture, Erastus Wiman named this
area and railroad station for himself in 1886 when he first
brought Buffalo Bill's Wild West Show to the Island.

FACTORYVILLE   Soon acquired its name from the dyeing and
printing factory established in 1819 by Barrett, Tileston and
Company.

FAYETTSVILLE   An early name for Graniteville.

FOX HILL   In the middle 1800s the estate of Lewis H. Meyer.
As Fox Hills the area was used as a U.S. Army Base Hospital
during World War I.

GARRETSON'S   Named for an early family granted large acreage
in the 1730s. The present Dongan Hills station was called Garretson's in the beginning.

GIFFORD'S   Long the name of the present Great Kills area.

GRANITEVILLE   Designated on 1850 maps. Named for nearby
GRANITE VILLAGE   quarries.

GRANT CITY   A development started after the Civil War. Because of numerous French families living there it was sometimes
called Frenchtown and New Paris.

GRASMERE   The name is credited to Erastus Wiman in 1886.

GREAT KILLS   Along with the name of Gifford's this area in the
1800s was called Clarendon and Newton.

GREEN RIDGE   Dutch and Huguenot settlers and a few English
farmed here as early as 1700. Also called Kleine Kill, Fresh
Kill and Marshland.

GRYMES HILL   Received its name from the Grymes family, arriving in 1836.

HARRISVILLE   An 1890 name for Sandy Ground, part of the village
of Rossville.

HOLLAND HOOK   On the northwest tip of the Island. Said to
have been named for Henry Holland who served Richmond
County in the Colonial Assembly.

HUGUENOT   When it became the name of a railroad station

Huguenot soon replaced the area's former name of Bloomingview.

IRON HILL "Yserberg" by the Dutch who were said to have
taken out iron ore in 1644. Present day Todt Hill.

KARLE'S NECK A late 1600 name for the long stretch of farm
and marshland in the present New Springville area.

KREISCHERVILLE Named for Balthasar Kreischer, who set up an
extensive brick factory here in 1854. Now Charleston.

LINOLEUMVILLE Obviously named for the factory making this
product. Earlier names were Long Neck and New Blazing Star.
Now Travis.

LIVINGSTON So designated as a railroad station in 1886. Formerly
Elliottville.

LONDON BRIDGE A name for Bull's Head during the Revolution.

LONG NECK Now Travis.

LOWVILLE The name in 1849. Now Elm Park.

MANOR OF BENTLEY Captain Christopher Billopp's vast estate on
the southwest section of the Island.

MANOR OF CASSILTOWNE Colonial Governor Thomas Dongan's
domain on the North Shore.

MARINERS' HARBOR Noted for its former oystering and wartime
shipbuilding on the North Shore.

MARSHLAND Briefly a post office in 1874 for Green Ridge.

MERSEREAU'S FERRY A post-Revolution name for Port Richmond.

NEW BLAZING STAR Shown on 1793 and 1797 maps for Travis.

NEW BRIGHTON Started in 1834, covered sections including
Brighton or Hamilton Park, between York and Franklin Avenues; Jackson Park at Franklin and Third Street; the Goose
Patch between Westervelt Avenue and Jersey Street; and a row
of houses on the west side of the latter street called Dutch
Block. For many years the present St. George area received all
mail from the New Brighton post office.

NEW DORP The first Nieue Dorp was at the foot of the present
New Dorp Lane. Stony Brook and a second Dover are said to
have been English designations of the 17th century for certain
portions of its present coverage. Other portions were Elm Tree,
Cedar Grove, Oceana, Oceanville near the beach. A small race
track known as Sea View Park was on the site of the present
railroad station.

NEW DUBLIN Egbertville.

NEW PARIS Grant City.

NEW SPRINGVILLE The same as Springville, part of the original
Karle's Neck.

NORTH SIDE   Early name for the lands in the North Shore and later the post office for the area until West New Brighton came into being in 1871.

OAKWOOD HEIGHTS   Sometimes shortened to Oakwood was first known as Club House and Court House for railroad stations.

OLD PLACE   An area laced with creeks and marshland on the Island's northwest portion. Once called Tunissen's Neck.

OLD TOWN   The Island's first permanent settlement in 1661 near the present South Beach.

PEANUTVILLE   An early nickname for Chelsea.

PHOENIXVILLE   A more elegant early name for Bull's Head.

PORT RICHMOND   The Reverend James Brownlee of the Reformed Church is credited with giving the area this name in the mid-1800s. Known as a model village it was noted for its well-kept streets and good government at the time of consolidation.

PRALLTOWN   This was Chelsea's name during the Revolution.

PRINCE'S BAY   Originally named for the bay below Seguine's Point prior to the Revolution. Later, adjoining land also received the name.

PROHIBITION PARK   The first name for the present Westerleigh.

QUARANTINE   The first Quarantine was near the Watering Place and Tompkinsville from 1799 to 1858. The present Quarantine station is on the waterfront at Rosebank.

RICHMOND   In 1700 known as "Cuckoldstown," by the Revolution, as the county seat, it had the more dignified name of Richmond or Richmond Town.

RICHMOND VALLEY   A railroad station adjacent to Tottenville.

ROSEBANK   Selected as the name of a railroad station and post office in the 1880s and now covering a large area.

ROSSVILLE   Named in honor of Colonel William E. Ross, before 1840. In Revolutionary days called Blazing Star.

ST. GEORGE   Legend has Erastus Wiman naming his ferry terminal for George Law, a friend.

SANDY GROUND   Mentioned as a settlement as early as 1779. In the 1840s, free negroes from Maryland settled in the village, south of Rossville, and were noted as oystermen.

SEASIDE   An old name for Eltingville.

SKUNK'S MISERY   An 1857 name for the west area between Pleasant Plains and Prince's Bay.

SMOKING POINT   An old name associated with Rossville.

SNUG HARBOR   As early as 1831 Sailors' Snug Harbor was erected on the North Shore as the home for retired mariners.

SOUTH SIDE   Another early name for Eltingville.

SPRINGVILLE Better known as New Springville.

STAPLETON A village laid out near the ferry landing in 1836 and named in honor of William J. Staples, one of the developers.

STONY BROOK As early as 1679 there were houses in the general present area of Amboy and Richmond Roads and Egbertville. By 1711 courts were held there.

SUMMERVILLE South of Old Place and Mariners' Harbor.

TIPPERARY CORNERS An older name for Egbertville.

TODT HILL Historians disagree as to origin of the name Todt or Toad. "Todt" meaning "Death" for an Indian massacre or for a burial place for the Dutch? Or "Toad" for the amphibian? Prior to the Revolution the hill was Yserberg or Iron Hill.

TOMPKINSVILLE Proudly named for Daniel D. Tompkins, Governor of New York, 1807–1817, Vice President of the United States, 1817–1825, the Island's most illustrious citizen. Formerly the site of the Watering Place.

TOTTENVILLE Named for the Totten family. The southernmost village of New York state.

TOWER HILL A portion of Port Richmond and a railroad station.

TRAVIS Its other designations have been Decker Town, Long Neck, New Blazing Star and Linoleumville.

VANDERBILT'S LANDING Part of Clifton, at the foot of the present Vanderbilt Avenue.

WATCHOGUE Also called Merrilltown.

WEST NEW BRIGHTON The name was designated as a post office in 1871. Other names for the area were North Side, Cityville, Factoryville and Castleton Landing. Now called West Brighton.

WEST QUARTER An early name for Rossville.

WILLOWBROOK A brook, a road and an area around the present Victory Boulevard and Willowbrook Road. Also the location of Willowbrook State School.

WOODROW Lying between the Arthur Kill Road and Drumgoole Boulevard.

WOODS OF ARDEN Named by Erastus Wiman in 1886 when he acquired the property, along the waterfront and inland, at Eltingville.

YOUNG IRELAND Another name used for Egbertville.

Bibliography

Anthon, John and Charles E. *Anthon's Notes*. Staten Island: Staten Island Institute of Arts and Sciences.

Bayles, Richard M. *History of Richmond County*. New York: L. E. Preston & Company, 1887.

Brodhead, J. R. *History of the State of New York*. New York: 1853–71.

Clute, John J. *Annals of Staten Island*. New York: Press of Chas. Vogt, 1877.

Davis, William T. *Conference or Billopp House*. Staten Island: Published under the Auspices of the Staten Island Historical Society, 1926.

———. *Days Afield on Staten Island*. Staten Island: Published by the Author, 1892.

——— and Leng, Charles W. *Staten Island and Its People*, 5 vols. New York: Lewis Historical Publishing Co., 1930.

——— and Leng, Charles W. *Staten Island Names, Ye Olde Names and Nicknames*. Staten Island: Proceedings of the Natural Science Association of Staten Island, 1896. Supplement, 1903.

———, Leng, Charles W. and Vosburgh, Royden Woodward *The Church of St. Andrew, Staten Island*. Staten Island: Published under the Auspices of the Staten Island Historical Society, 1925.

——— and Hine, Charles Gilbert *Legends, Stories and Folklore of Old Staten Island*. Part I, The North Shore. Staten Island: Published Under the Auspices of the Staten Island Historical Society, 1925.

DeVries, David Pietersz *Journals*. New York: New-York Historical Society, Collections 2, Series III.

DuBois, Theodora and Smith, Dorothy Valentine. *Staten Island Patroons*. Staten Island: Staten Island Historical Society, 1961.

Hampton, Vernon B. *Staten Island's Claim to Fame*. Staten Island: Richmond Borough Publishing and Printing Co., 1925.

Hine, Charles Gilbert *The Story and Documentary History of the Perine House*. Staten Island: Staten Island Antiquarian Society, 1915.

Historical Records Survey. *Transcriptions of Early Town Records of New York. The Earliest Volume of Staten Island Records, 1678–1813*. New York: 1942.

Jameson, J. Franklin (Edited by) *Narratives of New Netherland*. New York: Charles Scribner's Sons, 1909. Barnes & Noble, Inc., 1937

Melyn, Cornelis. *Melyn Papers*. New York: New York Historical Society. Collections, 1913.

Morris, Ira K. *Memorial History of Staten Island*. Staten Island: Published by the Author, 2 vols. 1898–1900.

New York Genealogical and Biographical Society Record, New-York Historical Society Collections. Abstracts of Wills.

O'Callaghan, E. B. *Documentary History of the State of New York*. Albany: Weed, Parsons & Co., Public Printers, 1849.

Smith, Dorothy Valentine. *The Clove and Its Valley*. Staten Island: Staten Island Historical Society, 1956.

Staten Island Chamber of Commerce Reports.

Staten Island Church Records.

Staten Island Historian, quarterly. Staten Island: Staten Island Historical Society, 1938–1970.

Staten Island Institute of Arts and Sciences Proceedings.

Steinmeyer, Henry G. *Staten Island 1524–1898*. Staten Island: Staten Island Historical Society, 1950.

Stillwell, John E. *Historical and Genealogical Miscellany.*, 1903–16.

Stokes. Isaac Newton Phelps. *Iconography of Manhattan Island*. Privately Printed, 6 vols., 1915–22.

Tysen, David J. *Happenings Before and After Staten Island Became Part of Greater New York*. Staten Island: Staten Island Chamber of Commerce, 1924.

Manuscripts in the collections of the New-York Historical Society, New York Genealogical and Biographical Society, New York Public Library, Staten Island Historical Society, Staten Island Institute of Arts and Sciences, private collections, and the following newspapers: *Richmond County Gazette, Staten Island Advance,* and the *Staten Islander.*

Index

Index 235

Kellogg, Dr. John H., 160
Kennedy, Charles W., 209
Kennedy, Mrs. T. Livingstone, 213
Kent, Rockwell, 197
Kieft, William, 8, 11-14
Kill van Kull, 30, 31, 38
Kingsley, Charles Rawson, Rev., 159
Kingsley, Florence Morse, 160
Kiviat, Abel, 209
Knox, Colonel, 69
Knyphausen, Wilhelm von, Baron, 88
Kolff, Cornelius G., 118, 193, 213
Kost, Frederick W., 197
Kroesen, Henderyck. *See* Cruser, Hendrick
Kruse, Garret, 39
Kruse, Hendrick 39

Labadie, Jean de, 24
LaBau, L. B., 114
Lafayette, General, 93, 100
La Guardia, Fiorello H., 192
Lake, Daniel. *See* Locke, Daniel
Lakeman, Abraham, 42
Lake Tysen farmhouse, 214
Landmarks Preservation Commission, 211
Latourette, Paul, 74
Latourette, Peter, 90
Lawrence, Richard, 57
Lawrence, William Hurd, 197
Leason, Percy, 197
Lehmitz, Ernest, 195
Leng, Charles W., 38, 104, 213
Leonowens, Anna, 124-125
Leslie, Frank, 164
Lind, Jenny, 203
Lindsay, John V., Mayor of New York, 215
Littel, Judge, 145
Livingston, Anson, 129-136
Livingston, Robert R., 106-107
Locke, Daniel, 41
Locke, Richard Adams, 196
Long, Charles W., 22
Loring, Mrs. Joshua, 65

Love, Edward L., 214
Lovelace, Francis, 21
Lovelace, Thomas, 40
Lowell, Charles Russell, 132
Lowell, James Russell, 130
Ludlow, William, 208
Luten, Walrave, 18
Lynch, Eddie. *See* Sutton, Willie
Lyons, Caleb, 208

McIntyre, Matty, 209
Mackall, Lawton, 197
Mackenzie, Aeneas, 36-37
Mackenzie, Ranold Slidell, General, 202
McMillen, Loring, 213
Manor of Bentley. *See* Conference House
Manor of Castletown, 30-32
Maretzek, Max, 203
Markham, Edwin, 160
Marshall, John, Chief Justice, 107
Martin, John, 196
Mason, Arthur, 196
Melyn, Cornelis, 12-17
Mercer, Hugh, 86-87
Merrell, Joseph F., J., 199
Merrell, Richard, 37
Merrill, Isaac (Ike), 180
Merrill, Richard, 180
Merrill, Tabitha, 181
Mersereau, Jacob, Colonel, 74-75
Mersereau, John, 72-75
Mersereau, Joshua, 73
Mersereau, Paul, 74
Metcalf, Henry, County Judge, 186
Meucci, Antonio, 153
Michau, Paul, 57
Miller Field, 218-219
Mills, William W., 194
Minton, Robert B., 132
Monckton, Robert, 54-55
Monroe, James, 99-100
Moody, Lady, colony of, 20
Moore, George, 200
Moore, Richard Channing, 203
Morgan, John, 37